# RSPCA

# COMPLETE
# DOG
# TRAINING
# MANUAL

# RSPCA
# COMPLETE
# DOG
# TRAINING
## MANUAL

### DR. BRUCE FOGLE

Training sequences by
PATRICIA HOLDEN WHITE

DORLING KINDERSLEY
LONDON • NEW YORK • STUTTGART

# A DORLING KINDERSLEY BOOK

PROJECT EDITOR Tracey Williams
ART EDITOR Tim Scott
MANAGING EDITOR Krystyna Mayer
MANAGING ART EDITOR Derek Coombes
DTP DESIGNER Doug Miller
PRODUCTION CONTROLLER Antony Heller
TRAINER Patricia Holden White

First published in Great Britain in 1994
by Dorling Kindersley Limited,
9 Henrietta Street, London WC2E 8PS

Reprinted 1995

A CIP catalogue record for this book is available
from the British Library

ISBN 0-7513-0075-6

Colour reproduced by Colourscan, Singapore
Printed and bound by Mondadori, Italy

## The RSPCA and Dog Care

The RSPCA – the Royal Society for the
Prevention of Cruelty to Animals – is a
charity that was founded in 1824 to
promote kindness and prevent cruelty to
animals. Although the RSPCA is most
commonly associated with dogs and cats,
it cares for all animals, including farm
animals, wildlife, and animals used for
research purposes. The Society carries out
its vital animal welfare work through its
team of 300 uniformed inspectors stationed
throughout England and Wales, and
through its nationwide network of animal
homes, welfare centres, and clinics. Many
of these establishments are run by
voluntary workers who belong to the 208
branches that are the backbone of the
Society. Education has always been an
important part of the RSPCA's work, and a
major focus is teaching people about the
responsibilities involved in keeping an
animal. Many of the problems with which
it deals are caused by thoughtless or
irresponsible pet owners.

Dogs are among the most popular pets,
but they are also the most frequent victims
of mistreatment by irresponsible owners. A
badly kept, untrained dog can also be a
menace to society. Ignorance is the cause
of many problems.

This book is essential reading for any
existing or would-be dog owner. It tells you
how to create the best environment for a fit
and happy dog and embark upon a
successful training programme.

Only by understanding your dog's
behaviour and needs can you be sure of
giving it the kind of life it deserves.

**Terence Bate**
*Chief Veterinary Officer*

# Contents

# Introduction

The dog evolved from its wolf ancestors over 10,000 years ago, and since that time it has lived and worked with humans. The natural inclinations of the wolf were exaggerated through controlled breeding, and lines of dogs evolved bearing distinct abilities. Breeds were created for specific purposes, such as hunting, herding flocks of livestock, guarding campsites, and fighting by our sides during battle.

### Canine evolution

In all regions of the northern hemisphere – the natural territory of the wolf – our distant relatives tamed the wolf and so produced the dog. In North America, the Innuit created sledge dogs, animals with powerful shoulders who were willing to pull heavy loads. In Asia, a variety of dogs emerged, ranging in size from heavy-boned war dogs like Mastiffs, to delicate companion dogs such as the Pekingese. Dogs with the ability to run swiftly were bred to chase game, thereby creating the root stock of the modern-day Afghan, Saluki, and Greyhound.

### Speciality breeds

Further south in Asia, smaller hunting dogs evolved: the Singing Dog and the Dingo. These animals accompanied the Aboriginals when they settled in Papua New Guinea and Australia. In Europe, too, the wolf was tamed. The spitz-type dogs of northern Europe served our ancestors' needs by chasing large game. Speciality hunting breeds emerged, such as the Elkhound, Deerhound, Irish Wolfhound, and Otter Hound. Coursing and digging dogs – experts at killing small animals – were bred selectively, and today's terriers are their descendants. In Africa, Basenjis evolved as silent hunting companions.

### Breeding the domestic dog

Generations of selective breeding resulted in dogs becoming even more specialized in their abilities to work for or with humans. Some scenting dogs were developed to follow air scent, and others to follow ground scent. Dogs were bred to fight with bears, bulls, or each other, for our amusement. With the invention of the gun came the emergence of sporting dogs. These canines would point to, flush out, or retrieve game.

### Canine companions

The role of the dog is still evolving, and many former canine roles have been lost. However, with the emergence of Kennel Clubs throughout the world during the last century, over 400 breeds of dog – each developed for a specific purpose – still exist. Today, most of these dogs serve a single purpose, that of companions to humans.

### Problems of contemporary canines

Dogs were bred to work, to use their mental and physical energy, and to concentrate, and be alert. However, many modern-day canines, although fed regularly, kept physically healthy, and protected from danger, really lead very boring lives.

### Leading a dull life

One of the consequences of this dull lifestyle is the development of behavioural problems. Neighbours complain because dogs howl. Owners find exercising their dogs frustrating because their pet persistently pulls on the lead, tries to attack other dogs, or chases cyclists. People who do not own dogs often find them – and their owners – unpleasant because owners let their dogs soil public places. These problems are not the dog's fault; they are our fault simply because we have not trained our pets properly.

### Canine euthanasia

One of the most disturbing statistics in veterinary medicine concerns the cause of death of dogs. In many regions of the world, the most common cause of death of dogs under 18 months old is not illness, disease or injury, but euthanasia. The most prevalent reason why owners decide that their dog should die is that the dog has a behavioural problem. Although specific breeds are associated with certain types of behaviour, most behavioural problems develop as a consequence of inadequate training.

### Training your dog

Dog training is neither a contest to see who is most powerful, nor an ego-boosting exercise. It is never necessary to use violence. It is, however, essential to use common sense, be lavish with rewards, and have fun. Good training is based upon mutual trust and respect.

### Learning to train

Certain instincts and behaviours have been exaggerated in some breeds. However, regardless of breed, each dog has its own personality, and the amount of training that is necessary varies with the individual. How your dog thinks is described in Chapter One. Training does not mean enrolling in weekly classes, although with good instruction, classes are an excellent way of teaching you how to train your dog. Training does not mean a daily trudge to a nearby park or field to put your dog through a series of exercises. Training is an attitude as much as an exercise. In Chapter One you will also learn how to use rewards and give commands and, most important of all, how to time your commands, rewards, and discipline properly.

### Early training

Chapter Two contains information on puppy training, including the value of crate training and house training, the importance of grooming, and basic obedience commands. It also gives advice on the kinds of equipment to use. By following these instructions you will give your dog an advantage in life, and increase the likelihood that for the next 10 to 15 years you will have a perfect canine companion.

### Personal training

More advanced training is discussed in Chapter Three. Each training exercise includes detailed instructions, illustrated with step-by-step photographs. Every dog is an individual. In varying degrees, each is interested in mental and physical stimulation, sex, guarding territory, eating, sleeping, and personal comfort. Its temperament, attention span, age, and sex influence its propensity towards training. Not all dogs respond to the same teaching methods, and training techniques sometimes need to be altered to suit the individual's personality. Just as training follows set patterns, problems also follow set patterns, and information on training dogs with different needs is included. As well as advising on basic obedience training, Chapter Three includes information on training your dog to hold, retrieve, speak, and use its paw. Introducing your dog to children, strangers, other dogs, and other animals is also discussed.

### Canine behavioural problems

Even with conscientious training, some dogs still develop bad habits or behavioural problems; these are dealt with in Chapter Four. This chapter includes a discussion on the difference between natural dog behaviours that humans find unacceptable, such as scent marking, and learned bad habits, like destroying homes when they are left alone.

### Causes and cures

Common canine bad habits, and advice on how to deal with them, are comprehensively covered in Chapter Four. The causes and cures of behavioural disorders such as pulling on the lead, not coming when called, chasing, different forms of aggression, nervousness and fear biting, car and sex problems, boredom, and eating difficulties are described. This chapter also contains advice on where to obtain information on more specialized training.

### Commitment is rewarding

It is not necessary to be a brilliant trainer to produce a well-mannered dog, but you must be committed to the task. Training involves making correct decisions about where your dog sleeps, what kind of toys your dog plays with, and when it is fed, as well as teaching basic commands. Training encourages your dog's natural skills, reinforces your status as leader, and teaches you how to understand your dog. Once you have achieved this understanding, you will discover that there is no other domesticated animal that offers such active, enjoyable, and rewarding companionship.

# CHAPTER ONE

# Your Dog's Mind

Dogs are similar to humans in some ways: they need companionship, as well as mental and physical stimulation, in order to achieve their potential. They respond to rewards and develop bad habits when they are bored. They are always learning, whether they are being "schooled" or not. However, dogs are not people in disguise. Every dog has its own unique personality, and intelligence, tolerance, and trainability vary with each individual. Through selective breeding, humans have accentuated some of the wolf's personality traits in some dogs and reduced others. The canine species is our best animal friend because dogs are so willing to live within a human "pack" and respond to our commands.

# How Your Dog Thinks

Your dog thinks in a very logical way, but canine logic is simpler than human logic. Like their wolf ancestors, dogs are pack animals. They respect and respond to their pack leader, and are primarily interested in survival and comfort. To a dog, survival means food. This is advantageous during training, because it means that tasty food snacks can be used as potent rewards for your dog's good behaviour. You can also incorporate the dog's natural desires to seek comfort, to play, and to have its own personal space into your training routine as rewards for its responsive behaviour.

**Original dog pack**
The domestic dog's behaviour corresponds to that of the wolf. Through selective breeding, humans have accentuated certain wolf behaviours and diminished others. Regardless of size or conformation, your dog is actually a domesticated wolf.

**Modern dog pack**
Pet dogs rarely have the opportunity to act as a true pack. Sledge dogs are an exception, but here there are two pack leaders – one canine and one human.

*Food is given to canine pack leader*

*Dog pack leader shows authority by rising above other dogs*

**Willing to obey**
Few dogs want to be pack leaders. The vast majority feel safe, secure, and content knowing that there is someone in command. Early obedience training reinforces this natural behaviour, and teaches puppies to respond to commands given by humans.

*Puppy receives reward for obeying command*

**Survival techniques**
Dogs are always learning, and their mental and physical activities are geared to survival. Rewarding action, such as successful scavenging, will increase unless you intervene and prevent the behaviour.

*Dog leans against its pack leader for security and comfort*

## Physical Aspects

### SMALL DOGS

Whereas large dogs compete for food from birth, and always regard it as a major reward, smaller dogs are not as dependent on food for survival. Humans created small breeds by actively choosing small members of litters – puppies that might not have survived without our help – and encouraging them to breed. Small breeds are more selective eaters than large ones, so they do not necessarily respond well to food rewards.

## Comfort seekers

Like humans, dogs enjoy the comforts of life. If you let a young puppy sit on the furniture in your home, it will always think it is allowed to sit there. You can avoid this problem by providing your dog with its own, comfortable personal space.

## Avoiding discomfort

It is rarely necessary to physically discipline a dog. Most dogs learn to change their ways to avoid milder indirect discipline, such as a squirt from a water pistol.

*Dense coat prevents loss of body heat*

### COAT DENSITY

Many dogs seek human contact for comfort, but breeds with dense coats can appear more independent than those with thin coats, preferring solitude simply because it is cooler.

## Personal space

Like wolves, dogs instinctively defend their pack's territory. Pet dogs learn to recognize the perimeters of their human family's territory, whether it is the car, the home, or the garden, and will often defend it.

## Mental stimulation

Dogs need mental as well as physical stimulation. Providing your dog with a small selection of unique toys to play with teaches it to chew only certain items.

## Social gatherings

Make sure that your puppy is properly socialized with other canines when it is young. If it is not, it may only feel secure with human companions when it matures.

## Rewarding good behaviour

Always reward good behaviour, but do not expect your dog to respond the first time you issue a command. However, dogs soon learn to associate certain words with specific reactions and rewards.

*Dog returns for its favourite toy.*

# Breed Differences

For at least 10,000 years, humans have been involved in dog breeding. Dogs were originally bred for their behaviours and abilities, and it is only in the last 200 years that they have been bred primarily for size, coat, and colour. By originally breeding for temperament, certain body shapes and coat densities were also selected. In perpetuating those characteristics, humans have also perpetuated breed differences in behaviour. Specific breeds are associated with certain aspects of behaviour, and some types of dog are more predisposed towards training than others.

**Herding breeds**

Collies, shepherd dogs, and cattle dogs evolved to work as teams with shepherds and farmers. Originally bred for their stamina and to nip at the heels of livestock, they are loyal and energetic dogs. They bark when they are excited and have a tendency to nip.

*Selective breeding has resulted in dense coat*

*Heavy bone structure provides anchorage for powerful muscles*

**Northern breeds**

The Nordic or spitz group of dogs includes the Husky, Elkhound, Japanese Akita, and Chow Chow. These dogs have powerful shoulders and dense coats, which they shed abundantly. They have tremendous stamina, and are quite independent and aloof.

**Guarding dogs**

Mountain dogs such as the Bernese and Pyrenean were bred to guard flocks of sheep in the absence of the shepherd. They are relaxed but independent canines, with a tendency to be overprotective. Breeds such as Dobermanns and Boxers were bred to protect the home.

**Sight hounds**

Greyhounds, Whippets, Deerhounds, Afghan Hounds, and Salukis are all built for speed. Sometimes aloof and distant, sight hounds are not overwhelmingly demonstrative dogs.

## Gundogs

Setters, pointers, spaniels, and especially retrievers, were all bred to be cooperative and to respond to human commands. As a result, they are often particularly affectionate dogs.

## Scent hounds

Bloodhounds, Basset Hounds, and Beagles were originally bred to follow scent, work in packs, and howl signals to their masters. They communicate well with other dogs, and are able to follow the weakest trails.

*Nose is large to capture scent*

## Terriers

Originally developed to chase small game and vermin, most terriers are small, robust diggers with powerful barks. They rarely back down when challenged, and are the breeds most likely to snap and nip.

## Companion dogs

Toy dogs such as Chihuahuas, Tibetan breeds, small poodles and spaniels, and bichons have always been bred for companionship. They thrive on affection and human contact.

*Coat needs frequent attention to prevent matting*

# Personality Types

Although each breed of dog has its own general personality profile, ultimately every dog is unique. While some dogs are extroverts and like to be the centre of attention, others are more submissive. Both types of dog can be well trained, but different approaches are needed. Where your dog has come from and what it has experienced early in life will also affect its ability to be trained, as will its sex. Neutered dogs and females between seasons are easiest to train, while unneutered male dogs are the least responsive.

## DIFFERENT PERSONALITIES

### Dominant and confident
Some dogs, regardless of breed, have naturally confident personalities. Male dogs tend to be more dominant and confident than females. The dominant dog is most likely to resist training.

### Submissive and insecure
Dogs with submissive personalities can be overwhelmed when commanded to obey. These dogs require a slow and gentle approach during training, so you should not issue commands too harshly.

*Dog cowers fearfully*

### Easily distracted
Some dogs are more interested in playing with other dogs than in obeying their owners. Often, these dogs were not properly socialized with people when they were puppies. It is best to train this type of dog on its own at first, rather than in a class.

*Owner issues command*

### Cooperative and responsive
The dogs that are easiest to train are those that have natural curiosity, and an affinity with humans. Dogs that investigate and listen to people respond most quickly to training.

*Dog concentrates on another dog*

## SOURCES OF DOGS

### Rescued dogs

Rescued dogs, especially mature ones, often arrive with unknown or unexpected behavioural problems. You should only adopt a dog from a rescue shelter if you are prepared to expend the time and energy that looking after it entails *(see page 86)*.

### Pet shops

Although many delightful dogs come through animal dealers, there is a greater likelihood of both disease and behavioural problems being present in these dogs than in those from breeders. Many of these problems are created by inadequate socialization during the critical early months of the dog's life. Lack of contact with people, periods of isolation, and unpleasant incidents with other canines can all affect a dog's eventual behaviour.

### Responsible breeders

You should ideally acquire a dog from a breeder who looks after the dogs' mental and physical health. Visit the breeder and ask to see the mother of the puppies and several other adult dogs.

## Personality Traits

### DOMINANCE

Some dogs are extremely dominant, and display their dominance by using intimidating body language, staring, holding their tail high, and even baring their teeth and barking in a threatening way. When training a dog with this type of personality, you should definitely seek professional help.

### SUBMISSION

At the other end of the personality scale are dogs that are intensely submissive. They avoid eye contact, tuck their tails between their legs when their owner issues a command, and collapse in fear when anyone approaches them. If your dog behaves in this way, and if you have never trained a dog before, consider seeking professional help.

### COMPROMISE

The vast majority of dogs are neither dominant nor submissive. In some circumstances and with some individuals they are dominant and in other circumstances or with other individuals they are submissive. Most dogs have a mixture of both behaviours in their personalities.

### MANIPULATION

Some dogs cleverly dominate their owners by claiming to be helpless and submissive. A dog that does this may scratch at its owner's legs and demand to be picked up, or refuse to eat its food. These manipulators are dominant individuals that have learned different methods of showing authority.

### PECKING ORDER

In a household, the pet dog should learn that it must obey all human members of its family. It should understand that under some circumstances, for example when it hears a noise outside the window, it may express its natural dominance by barking a warning. In other circumstances, for example when a human member of the household gives a command, it must obey.

# Early Learning

By the time you acquire your dog, its behaviour will have been influenced by its mother, and by its relationship with its littermates. For example, if a mother barks to attract attention, her puppies are likely to behave in the same way. Experiences that occur between three and twelve weeks of age are critical in the development of a dog's personality. The best time to acquire a puppy is when it is about eight weeks old. By ensuring that it gains as much varied experience as possible during the following month, you will lay the groundwork for easy, productive, and rewarding training.

*Puppy fearlessly examines new faces*

### Meeting people
Make sure that the new puppy meets as many people as possible while it is still very young. With your vet's permission, take the puppy in the car, to work, and to friends' homes whenever possible. Let the puppy play with dogs that you know are healthy, and introduce it to children and other adults.

### Personal investigation
Playing with toys will provide the puppy with mental and physical stimulation. Find out which toys the puppy prefers (making sure that they are unlike other domestic articles), and use them as rewards during training.

*Puppy eagerly takes part in play activity*

### Play constructively

You can play active games with the puppy, but you should always be in control of these. While you play, watch the puppy's behaviour, and if it is about to sit, issue a "Sit" command.

### Give immediate rewards

When the puppy obeys a command, offer an immediate reward, such as stroking or soothing words. As the dominant member of the partnership, you should always be in control.

*Puppy enjoys being stroked*

### Early habits endure

If you carry a puppy constantly when it is very young, it will expect similar treatment when it feels insecure as an adult.

---

## Social Development

### SOCIAL GATHERINGS

Dogs must learn to behave properly, both with their own species and with others, especially humans. This is a difficult task, and the best time for them to learn is when they are very young – under four months old. Whenever possible, make sure that the puppy meets other species such as cats and horses when it is very young. Early socialization to other species reduces the likelihood of future problems. With the advice of your vet or local dog training club, organize or participate in supervised weekly puppy evenings *(see page 122)*. At these gatherings, puppies learn how to respond to other dogs and to strangers.

### SOCIAL DEPRIVATION

Dogs that lack early social experiences can be difficult to train. Restricted contact with humans during puppyhood can create limitations in the dog's ability to obey commands. Before acquiring a dog, find out as much as possible about its early experiences. The more a puppy has been handled, the more likely it is to respond to training. Puppies raised with little human contact can be very challenging to train; they often need extra attention, and professional assistance is sometimes necessary.

---

*Puppy instinctively knows that it is being dominated*

### Give mental stimulation

Puppies that are actively stimulated at between three and twelve weeks of age grow into adults that are adept at both learning and problem solving. A puppy learns best by observing its mother's behaviour. Within a human family, one person should be the "mother substitute", who should be responsible for training the puppy, although all other family members should participate.

### Understanding fear

Oversee all the puppy's activities, to ensure that frightening situations are kept to a minimum. Fears learned at an early age can become lifelong phobias unless they are rapidly overcome.

# Rewards and Discipline

Dogs need constant encouragement when they are being trained. Food snacks, toys, and physical contact and verbal praise from their owners are all strong rewards.

Physical punishment should not be used to discipline a dog. Instead, immediately after your dog misbehaves, isolate it for a few minutes, or give it an unpleasant surprise.

## TYPES OF REWARD

**Tasty treats**
Hold a food treat above the dog's nose to attract its attention. This works best when the dog is hungry.

*Reward is held in palm of hand*

*Even strokes are given with a flat palm*

**Contact comfort**
Physical rewards are important during training, so praise the dog by giving it long strokes along its body.

**Rewarding toys**
As an incentive, show the dog its favourite toy. You will soon discover which toys it likes best.

*Eye contact is made by holding toy above dog's head*

## SUITABLE REWARDS

CHICKEN-FLAVOURED SNACKS

BEEF BONES

BEEF CHUNKS

MIXED-FLAVOUR SNACKS

CHEESE-FLAVOURED BISCUITS

LIVER AND GARLIC TREATS

COLOURED CHEW STICKS

THROW BALL

DRIED FOOD

CHEW TOY

SQUEAKY BALL

EASY-GRIP TOY

PLASTIC RING

RUBBER BONE

SQUEAKY TOY

WAIST BAG FOR CARRYING EQUIPMENT

Every dog has its own personal preferences for snack foods and toys. Observe the dog's behaviour and learn what it likes best, then only give these special treats as rewards for good behaviour. Food rewards work for most dogs, but some individuals may prefer toys. During training sessions, keep snacks and small toys in a waist bag or pocket for convenience.

# TYPES OF DISCIPLINE

**Lonely miscreant**
If the dog misbehaves, isolate it from household activity. This is suitable discipline, since most dogs enjoy human companionship. Isolation should only last for a few minutes, and should be followed immediately by calm release.

## Common Mistakes

IMPROPER REWARDS
Patting a dog on the head is a dominant gesture, and should never be used as a reward. Instead, stroke the dog along the side of its body.

TOO MANY TOYS
If a dog is provided with too many toys, it may think it can chew anything. Allow a maximum of three toys that are unlike any household items.

UNEXPECTED REWARDS
This dog is scavenging in a rubbish bin. Avoid situations where the dog receives unplanned rewards like this.

*Isolated dog howls at closed door*

"LEAVE IT"

*Owner uses water pistol to reinforce spoken command*

**Harsh words**
A verbal command, together with an unexpected and unpleasant – but harmless – squirt from a water pistol, is an effective way of reprimanding the dog if it misbehaves.

*Dog reaches out to take food, not expecting discipline*

# Perfect Timing

When you begin training, make sure your dog knows that rewards are at hand. Praise and reward your dog the instant it responds to your commands. Once your dog has learned your word and hand signals, begin to give fewer food rewards. Never reprimand your dog after it has misbehaved, since it will not know why you are angry.

**Eye contact**
Give verbal commands and hand signals only when you have eye contact with the dog. Do not overstimulate the dog by using too many food rewards *(see below).*

"STAY"

**Body language**
Anticipate the dog's behaviour by observing its body language. Give commands when you notice that the dog is beginning to lose concentration, and not after it disobeys you.

"WAIT"

*Food reward is used with hand signal and verbal command*

*Dog loses concentration*

*Reward is given as soon as dog returns*

**Instant rewards**
Reward the dog as soon as it complies with your command. At first, combine food rewards with verbal praise. After a while, give fewer food rewards but always give either physical or verbal praise.

## Anticipating behaviour

Command the dog to stay the moment it makes eye contact with another dog, and before it raises its hackles, growls, or begins to pull on the lead.

*Owner is ready to turn dog's head away*

## Unplanned reward

As this dog chases, the cyclist rides away and the dog wrongly receives an instant, satisfying, and well-timed reward. The timing of the reward reinforces the behaviour.

*Dog pants with excitement of chase*

## Common Mistakes

### SEVERAL DOGS

Training several dogs at once should only be attempted by professional dog trainers. You should only train one dog at a time, while keeping the other dogs out of sight.

### INAPPROPRIATE DISCIPLINE

*Dog does not understand why its owner is angry*

Reprimand the dog only when you actually observe it misbehaving. Displaying anger after the event will simply confuse the dog.

*Begging is unacceptable behaviour and should not be reinforced*

### REINFORCEMENT

Rewarding the dog intermittently is the most effective way of reinforcing behaviour, but you should only reinforce good behaviour.

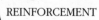

# Giving Commands

Dogs respond best to short, sharp commands, given with obvious hand signals. Avoid constantly repeating a command, since this will confuse your dog. Attract your pet's attention by speaking its name, then give your command. The inflection in your voice is important, as are facial expressions. Smile when you are pleased, and scowl at the dog if it wilfully disobeys your command.

"ROVER"

"ROVER COME"

*Arms held wide to welcome recalled dog*

**Attracting attention**
Use the dog's name to attract its attention. Stand upright, with your shoulders back, and keep the dog's concentration focused on you. Show the dog the food reward as an incentive.

**Welcoming body language**
Encourage the dog to respond to you by assuming a welcoming posture. Smile, use a friendly and exciting tone of voice, and open your arms to receive the dog.

*Holding treat in clenched fist prevents dog from snapping*

" NO "

*Command is given as dog begins to raise its paws*

**Firm words**
When disciplining the dog, lower your voice and say "No" sharply. Some dogs respond best to the lower tone of a man's voice.

## Stern body language

When the dog misbehaves, assume a threatening posture, and look angry when using negative commands like "No". You should seek professional advice if you have a particularly dominant dog that disobeys you persistently.

*Owner's stance is threatening to dog*

*"SIT"*

*Dog learns that owner's right arm raised at elbow means "Sit"*

*Dog watches and listens*

## Hand signals

Teach the dog to respond to a combination of spoken and visual commands. When the dog is some distance away from you, you can control it by calling its name, then using dramatic hand signals.

## Additional Information

### UNDERSTANDING LANGUAGE

Dogs have a limited ability to understand the human language. They respond best to short, sharp words. To avoid confusion, choose a one- or two-syllable name for the dog, making sure that it is unlike other common words. Do not constantly repeat commands, since this is confusing to dogs. Choose a simple word like "Free" or "OK" as the release from a command.

### THE VALUE OF "NO"

"No" is one of the most important words a dog will learn, since it can prevent it from doing something dangerous. The timing of your commands, and knowing when to say "No", are important elements of dog training. If a shy dog backs away from a stranger, and you try to reassure it by saying "It's OK", you are actually telling it that you approve of its behaviour. Instead, say "No" firmly.

### BODY LANGUAGE

Dogs are adept at reading human body language. The dog will notice when you are losing concentration or becoming bored with the training session. Be generous with your praise, and dramatic when you reprimand the dog. Always try to maintain the dog's attention by being alert during training.

# Putting It All Together

Training should be enjoyable for both you and your dog. Begin training in a quiet environment, and increase the distractions over several weeks, until the dog behaves well in any environment. Keep the sessions short, only train when you and your dog are alert, and never issue commands you cannot enforce. End each session on a positive note.

*Dog is too tired to train*

### Short lessons

Dogs have shorter attention spans than humans. You should train the dog for a maximum of 15 minutes, twice a day. Do not attempt to train if either you or the dog are not concentrating.

### Primary rewards

Although snacks are good rewards, you should avoid using particularly tasty ones to prevent the dog from concentrating on the treat rather than on training. Some dogs respond better to squeaky toys, but do not use these if the dog runs away with them.

"SIT"

*Food is effective reward for hungry dog*

### Optimum time

It is best to train when the dog is hungry. It will be mentally alert, and will respond best to food rewards. Giving a dog two meals a day creates time for two good training sessions.

*Reward obedience with dry titbits*

"SIT"

### Less potent rewards

Over a few days, reduce the frequency of edible and physical rewards, but always give verbal praise. The dog will soon learn to respond to verbal praise alone.

*Dog sits to verbal command alone*

## Training outdoors

Once the dog reliably obeys commands in the quiet environment of your home, move to a quiet location outdoors and repeat the training sessions. Make sure you are always in a position of control, so that you are able to enforce your commands.

"SIT"

*Dog is on lead and under owner's control*

## Busy environments

Once the dog is obedient both indoors and in quiet outdoor locations, graduate to a busier area.

"SIT"

*Dog responds to command in presence of another dog*

## Enforcing commands

Only give commands if you know you are in control. This dog has been distracted, but because it is on a lead the owner knows she can enforce compliance if the food lure and verbal command are disregarded.

"COME LIBERTY"

*During indoor and outdoor training, dog wears long training lead*

## Finish with fun

Always finish training with something the dog enjoys and is able to do. Play with the dog, but do not save the greatest rewards for the end of the training session. If you do, the dog will want to end the exercise quickly in order to receive its final reward.

## Training is not exercise

Dogs need exercise, and time to play with other dogs. Training is not a substitute for either of these, so ensure that the dog gets the exercise its age, breed, and temperament require.

# Early Training

**D**ogs learn best when they are young and willing, and have not learned any bad habits. Do not wait until your puppy is six months old before teaching it basic commands; you should begin training the day your new companion arrives in your home. Provide your puppy with a well-fitting collar, its own private place to sleep and play in quietly, and suitable toys. Base your initial training programme around the puppy's feeding schedule, by teaching simple commands and rewarding it with its food allowance. Within days, most puppies will come to you and sit on command every time their food is prepared. Make sure your puppy meets other people and animals – under controlled circumstances – while it is young. At an early stage, introduce it to what will be the routines of its later life.

# Early Home Routines

It is best to start training as soon as you bring a new puppy into your home. Teach the puppy your rules before it starts to make its own. All family members should routinely handle a new puppy while it learns to wear a collar and lead, eat only from its own food bowl, sleep in its own bed, come when called, and wait on command. However, only one member of the family should be responsible for actually training the puppy.

### Learning respect
A puppy must learn to obey the family in its new home, so all responsible family members should handle the puppy.

*Puppy wears collar and identification tag*

*Puppy wears a houseline, ensuring that owner is in control*

### Learning to wait
The puppy should learn that people eat before dogs, and are therefore more dominant.

### Positive enticement
Using food enticement rather than discipline, teach the puppy which activities are not allowed.

*Food is held low, while owner commands "Off"*

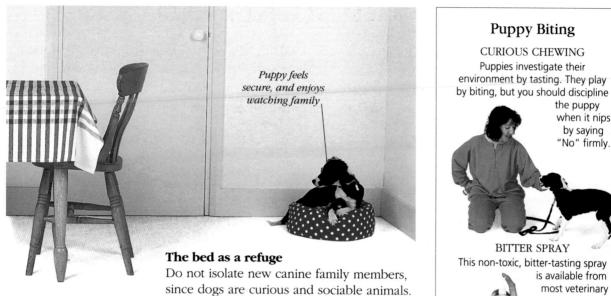

*Puppy feels secure, and enjoys watching family*

### Puppy Biting

**CURIOUS CHEWING**
Puppies investigate their environment by tasting. They play by biting, but you should discipline the puppy when it nips by saying "No" firmly.

**BITTER SPRAY**
This non-toxic, bitter-tasting spray is available from most veterinary surgeries.

*Apply spray to objects that you do not want dog to chew*

### The bed as a refuge

Do not isolate new canine family members, since dogs are curious and sociable animals. Set up a dog bed as a personal space for the puppy, and place it in a busy area of the home, such as a corner of the kitchen.

### People go first

Dogs naturally want to rush through doors first. By teaching a puppy to wait and allow you to go first, you are asserting your authority over it. If the puppy does not understand this relationship, training can be difficult.

### A private place

Train the puppy to enjoy being left in a crate with its toys *(see page 34 )*, leaving it alone for short periods at first. The crate can be moved to your bedroom at night.

"WAIT"

*Puppy on lead waits while owner goes through door*

# Basic Equipment

Choose accessories that are appropriate for the size and temperament of your dog, and replace collars frequently as your puppy grows. You will need a short lead, a long training lead, and an equally long, light houseline to use at home. Body harnesses, head halters, and muzzles are useful for certain types of dog *(see pages 54–55)*.

## COLLARS

REFLECTIVE BUCKLE COLLAR

LARGE LEATHER AND NYLON BUCKLE COLLAR

SMALL LEATHER AND NYLON BUCKLE COLLAR

PUPPY COLLAR WITH IDENTITY TAG

SMALL PUPPY COLLAR

LARGE ADJUSTABLE WRAP-AROUND COLLAR

MEDIUM ADJUSTABLE WRAP-AROUND COLLAR

HALF-CHECK COLLAR

SMALL ADJUSTABLE WRAP-AROUND COLLAR

CHECK CHAIN

### All shapes and sizes

Collars are usually made of nylon, cotton, or leather, and vary in size, quality, and price. You should be able to slip two fingers under a well-fitting collar. Simple buckle collars are best for many dogs, but half-check collars are ideal for boisterous individuals with short attention spans *(see page 54)*. Check chains are useful when used properly, but are dangerous on breeds with soft windpipes, such as Yorkshire Terriers.

## LEADS

LEATHER LEAD

2-METRE (6-FT) COTTON-WEBBING LEAD

EXTENDING LEAD

### The long and the short

You should always have your dog under your control, and this is particularly important during training. In addition to a standard lead, use a long cotton lead for outdoor training, and a long houseline with a bolt snap for indoor control. Make sure that the lead and bolt snap are not too heavy for your dog. Extending leads are practical, since they allow the dog some freedom, while you still have control.

6-METRE (20-FT) COTTON-WEBBING LEAD

NYLON CORD LONGLINE

NYLON CORD HOUSELINE

# HEAD HALTERS AND HARNESSES

HEAD HALTER

FIGURE-OF-EIGHT HEAD COLLAR

ADJUSTABLE HEAD HALTER

HEAD HALTER ADAPTER

## Complete control
Head halters *(see page 55)* are ideal for fearful, bold, and independent dogs, as well as for those that mouth and chew excessively. The lead clips to a ring under the dog's jaw. If the dog pulls forwards, its own momentum pulls its jaws shut and its head down. Use a body harness on dogs with small heads or weak windpipes *(see page 54)*.

BODY HARNESS

## MUZZLES

### Bite-prevention
Muzzles might appear unpleasant to you, but dogs quickly learn to wear them. Besides their obvious use on potentially aggressive dogs, they are ideal for preventing destructive dogs from chewing, and for stopping dogs that are prone to scavenging from eating unsavoury items. Basket muzzles permit barking and even panting, but a muzzle should not be left on your dog if no one is there to supervise it.

BASKET MUZZLE

## Additional Equipment

BEAN-BAG BED

PUPPY PLAYPEN

CRATE

### HAVENS FOR DOGS
Bean bags make excellent beds, while newspaper-lined playpens provide for playful activity and controlled house training. Crates should only be used for sleeping and quiet play.

### LIFEJACKET
Dogs swim naturally, but are at risk from drowning if they become exhausted. Dogs should wear lifejackets when they are on boats.

### BACKPACK
Physically fit dogs that accompany their owners on hiking or camping trips can carry their own food and bowls in special backpacks.

# Crate Training

It might look like a jail to you, but to the dog that has been trained from puppyhood to use it, a crate becomes a favourite place, the dog's own secure haven. Crates should be pleasant places and should never be used for discipline. Crate training encourages house training, reduces potentially destructive behaviour, and eases travelling with your dog.

*Fresh water should be provided in a non-tip bowl*

1 Before starting crate training, place soft bedding, a bowl of water, and an interesting toy inside the crate. Leave the door open initially.

2 Using a tasty snack, and the verbal command "Go to your crate", entice the puppy into its new home. Ensure that the door remains open so that the puppy can leave the crate at any time.

*Puppy willingly enters its personal "den"*

3 Once the puppy has become accustomed to the crate, it will continue to use it without any prompting from you.

4 While the puppy plays contentedly, close the crate door for a few minutes. Keep the crate in a busy place like the kitchen.

*Puppy plays vigorously with toy*

## Added Benefits

*Puppy is relaxed and feels secure*

*Crate offers safety in case of an accident*

**PERSONAL TRANSPORT**
Problems with travelling are eased if you have a crate-trained puppy. When confined to its own crate, this puppy feels secure in the car.

**PEN-FRIENDS**
If the playpen is lined with newspaper, puppies can meet and play without causing havoc in your home.

5 The relaxed puppy falls asleep in the security of its crate. Fully crate-trained puppies should not be left in crates for more than two hours during the day, and should be exercised before confinement.

## PUPPY PLAYPEN

Having become accustomed to its crate, this puppy is content to be confined to a playpen. Some dogs, especially rescued ones, will not tolerate crate confinement, but this rarely happens with puppies.

# House Training

Some dogs can be house trained quickly, while others take much longer. If you have an adult dog that has never been house trained, treat it as you would a new puppy. Never punish your dog for making a mess in your home. Reprimanding your pet after it has had an accident only teaches it to be nervous, and wary of you. Instead, anticipate when your dog needs to eliminate. After your dog wakes up, eats, or plays, take it to the place that you have chosen for it to relieve itself, and always clean up after it. Avoid accidents in the home by restricting your dog to its crate *(see page 34)*, until you have taken it out to eliminate. As your dog relieves itself, use words like "Hurry up", then praise it. Soon your dog will eliminate when you give the "Hurry up" command.

*An alarm will remind you to take puppy to its toilet area*

### Timing
Dogs actively avoid soiling their personal quarters. Restrict the puppy to its crate whenever you are busy, and provide it with a toy to chew. Carefully monitor the puppy's crate time, taking it out to relieve itself when necessary. Make sure that the crate is the correct size for the puppy; if it is too big the puppy may soil it.

### Paper training
Training the puppy to use newspaper indoors can be confusing to it, since it learns that eliminating indoors is acceptable. Whenever possible, train the puppy to eliminate in an outdoor area, but when circumstances dictate that you use paper indoors, follow the same crate restrictions, and let the puppy out on to its newspaper.

## Anticipation

A dog that suddenly puts its nose down and sniffs intently is usually signalling that it is about to eliminate. Commercial spray products, which induce the puppy to use a designated area, are available from most pet stores.

*Puppy sniffs just before urinating*

*Food, touch, and verbal rewards are given*

## Instant praise

When taking the puppy outside, keep its attention on you by talking to it or showing it toys, to ensure that there are no accidents on the way. Say "Hurry up" as the puppy eliminates, then praise it for its good behaviour.

## Create routines

A puppy will need to eliminate after sleeping and playing, and especially after eating or being restricted to its crate. As a general rule, remember that a three-month-old puppy needs to eliminate every three hours.

## Owner Training

### POINTLESS PUNISHMENT

Control your temper while you are house training a puppy. Scolding the dog is pointless unless you actually see it eliminating indoors. If you do, say "No" sternly, and move the puppy to its designated spot.

*Dog cowers as owner scolds it*

Prevent accidents from occurring by constantly supervising the puppy. If direct supervision is not possible, it is best to keep the puppy in its crate.

### RESPONSIBLE BEHAVIOUR

Dog faeces are not only a public health hazard to people and to other dogs, but also an aesthetic hazard to the environment. Ensure good relations with the community by always cleaning up after the dog. When you take the dog to a public place, remember to carry a poop scoop like the one below, or a simple plastic bag.

*Bag is pulled over handle*

*Use biodegradable bags when possible*

# Daily Grooming

Grooming your dog daily not only keeps it clean and healthy, but also reasserts your authority over it. Picking up the dog, holding its head, and opening its mouth are dominant gestures, and help to reinforce your control. Initially, use food rewards as distractions throughout the grooming sessions, then progress to verbal and physical praise alone.

## GROOMING EQUIPMENT

**Clipping utensils**
Fast-growing coats require clipping or cutting, while heavy coats often need to be thinned out. Train the dog from an early age to accept the sounds of clippers and scissors. Nails, especially those of small, lightweight, or elderly dogs, need frequent attention.

**Teeth and ear utensils**
Unless there is disease present, a puppy's teeth and ears are naturally clean. Later in life, however, these parts of the body benefit from routine cleaning. Train the dog while it is young to permit you to attend to these areas.

**Brushes and combs**
Brushing the dog daily keeps its coat in top condition. It also reminds the dog that you are in control. Always use equipment appropriate for the dog's coat type.

NAIL CUTTERS
ELECTRIC CLIPPERS
THINNING SCISSORS
CUTTING SCISSORS
TOOTHBRUSH
CANINE TOOTHPASTE
COTTON WOOL
COTTON-WOOL BUDS
TOOTH-TARTAR REMOVER
EAR FORCEPS
SLICKER BRUSH
RUBBER BRUSH
PIN BRUSH
FLEA COMB
SOFT PIN BRUSH
SYNTHETIC BRISTLE BRUSH
CHAMOIS CLOTH
STRIPPING COMB
WIDE-TOOTHED COMB
NARROW-TOOTHED COMB

## GROOMING PREPARATIONS

*Dog is on lead for assured control*

**Picking up a dog**
Pick up the dog by putting one arm around its chest and forelimbs, and the other around its rump. Place it on a table for grooming.

**Holding a dog still**
Hold the dog in the stand position, and put your thumb through its collar.

*Hand is placed, palm down, under dog's body*

*Rubber mat is a useful, non-slip surface*

### Trimming the nails

It is easiest to cut the nails after the dog has been bathed, when its nails will be softer than usual. Take care not to cut the living tissue (the pink area inside the nail). If in doubt, seek veterinary advice.

*Clippers cut white tip of nail*

### Cleaning the eyes

Many dogs build up mucus in the corners of their eyes. Holding the head firmly, bathe the eyes, using a clean piece of damp cotton wool for each one. Eye cleaning is best carried out when the dog understands the "Sit" and "Stay" commands *(see page 56).*

*Holding head firmly is a dominant gesture*

### Examining the mouth

Use food rewards while training the dog to let you open and examine its mouth. You should check the dog's teeth and gums once a week.

*Jaw is held gently but firmly*

### Gentle brushing

Use long, firm strokes to brush along the dog's body. Brush the entire coat, including the tail and legs.

### Turning a dog around

Place the flat of your hand, with the fingers together, over the hind-leg muscles, to turn the dog around.

*Flat palm avoids hurting dog*

## Special Conditions

### LONG COATS

*Owner uses slicker brush*

Longhaired dogs with thick coats can develop matts under the legs. Take care when grooming these areas, since the skin here is often more sensitive than on other parts of the dog's body.

### LIPS AND GUMS

Some breeds need to have their lip folds cleaned, and their gums checked regularly. Use damp cotton-wool buds to remove any dirt.

### HAIRY EARS

Use a damp cotton-wool bud to clean the ears. Carefully remove excess hair using forceps or your fingers.

### FOOT MAINTENANCE

Minimize the risk of dirt embedding between the toes, by clipping and examining after exercise.

# Coming to You

Begin this exercise when your puppy is alert and hungry. Divide your pet's meal into ten equal portions, and throughout the day entice it to the food bowl by using its name and the command "Come". You should never recall the puppy to discipline it, since it will associate returning to you with the unpleasant experience of being reprimanded.

## INDOOR TRAINING

*"POLLY COME"*

**1** Stand a short distance away from the puppy, in a quiet room with no distractions. A hallway is an ideal location. With food visible in your hand, speak the puppy's name, and as it begins to move forwards give the command "Come".

*Puppy makes eye contact with owner*

*Food held out to entice puppy*

**3** As the puppy approaches, kneel down to get closer to its level. Praise the puppy again with words, stroking, and the food reward.

*"GOOD DOG"*

**2** As the puppy comes to you, praise it by saying "Good dog" in an enthusiastic voice. Encourage the puppy to come to you by bending your knees and opening your arms.

*Treat is given immediately puppy returns*

*Bent knees bring treat closer to puppy*

## OUTDOOR TRAINING

*Puppy is distracted by other dogs*

*Puppy can feel pressure on lead*

**1** When the puppy is fully trained to come to you indoors, move to a more distracting location. Keep the puppy on a longline or extending lead to ensure compliance, and repeat the exercise.

*"GOOD DOG"*

**2** Do not use the lead to reel in the puppy; encourage the puppy to return for its reward. A quick jerk on the lead can attract the puppy's attention if it is losing concentration. From a distance, a toy reward is more visible to the puppy than a food reward.

### Problem Solving

#### THE SLEEPY DOG

Dogs – and puppies in particular – have short attention spans, and training is mentally exhausting for them. Train for only five to fifteen minutes at a time, and never train when the dog is tired. You should also plan training periods to occur before the dog embarks on active exercise, so that it is physically and mentally prepared for the session. Vary the places in which you train the dog, so that you maintain its interest.

#### THE DISTRACTED DOG

If the dog does not respond to a food reward, alter its feeding routine, giving fewer meals (but larger quantities). If it still does not respond well to food treats, try using a favourite squeaky toy as a reward.

*Squeaky toy attracts puppy's attention*

#### THE WILFUL DOG

If the puppy is strong willed, always carry out any training exercise with it on a lead. This ensures that you can always attract the puppy's attention, and reminds it that it must listen and respond.

*"COME"*

# Sit and Lie Down

Once your puppy responds well to the command to come *(see page 40)*, you can teach it to sit and to lie down. You should practise this exercise with the puppy on the lead, to ensure that you are in control. On completing this routine successfully, your puppy will be able to carry out a sequence of commands for the first time.

## THE "SIT" COMMAND

1 Facing the puppy, move away with the lead in your left hand and a food treat in your right. As you command the puppy to come to you, show it the food. It is important to be calm, and not to excite the puppy during this exercise.

*Food is held in front of middle of body*

"SIT" "GOOD DOG"

*Food is held directly above puppy's head*

2 When the puppy reaches you, slowly move your right hand up and over its head. The puppy will naturally sit down in order to keep its eyes on the food. Give the command "Sit" when you see the puppy begin to bend its hind legs.

*Puppy tucks hindquarters into sitting position*

3 Reinforce the sit command from the front and then to the side of the puppy. At first, reward each response with verbal praise and food treats. Gradually reduce the food rewards – eventually words alone will be sufficient.

# THE "DOWN" COMMAND

**1** With the puppy in the sit position, kneel at its right side and hold its collar in your left hand. Holding a food treat in your right hand, place it on the puppy's nose and start to move it downwards.

**2** As the puppy's nose follows the treat, move it forwards in front of its body. The moment the puppy starts to lie down, give the command "Down".

*Lead is attached to collar and held firmly under knees*

*Food is held in clenched fist to prevent snatching*

"DOWN"

*Puppy moves head to maintain contact with treat*

"GOOD DOG"

**3** Continue to move the food forwards until the puppy is lying down. Reward the puppy with praise and the food treat. Repeat the exercise frequently, until the puppy responds to words alone.

## Problem Solving

### REFUSING TO SIT DOWN

If the puppy will not sit for a food reward, kneel down and hold its collar with your right hand, and tuck its hindquarters under with your left. Give the command "Sit" as you do this, then reward the puppy with praise.

*Fingers held together to avoid hurting puppy*

### REFUSING TO LIE DOWN

Kneel down with the puppy sitting on your left side. Placing your right palm under the puppy's right foreleg, and your left palm under its left foreleg, raise it to a begging position. Lower the puppy into a lying position, and reward it with praise.

*Hands do not grip legs*

### REFUSING TO STAY DOWN

*Fingers are kept together over shoulder muscle*

If the puppy tries to jump up before it has completed the exercise, apply gentle pressure over its withers. After a few seconds, release the puppy, saying "OK".

# Walking without a Lead

Outdoor activities are a delight when your dog walks obediently by your side. It is often easiest to train a puppy to walk to heel off the lead at first, since it will enjoy human companionship and will usually be willing to follow its owner. Most puppies will also follow the scent of food snacks, so it is useful to carry treats throughout training.

**1** With the puppy on your left side, hold its collar with your left hand and keep a food treat in your right hand. Attract the puppy's attention by speaking its name.

*"PRINCE"*

**2** Walking in a straight line, with the puppy following the food reward, give the command "Heel". Keep your left hand low, ready to grasp the puppy's collar.

*"HEEL"*

*Scent of food attracts puppy*

*Arm prevents unwanted movement*

*Puppy concentrates on potential reward*

**3** Give the command "Wait", and kneel to the puppy's right side, holding the snack low down to discourage jumping. Your left hand, palm down, underneath the puppy's body prevents it from moving.

**4** Bending your knees and holding the food near to the puppy's nose, make a right turn, repeating the "Heel" command. The puppy must speed up to walk around you.

*Arm draws puppy to the right*

" H E E L "

*Puppy follows treat intently*

" S T E A D Y "

**5** To make a left turn, use your left hand to guide the puppy by the collar, and give the command "Steady". Hold the food reward low down and move your right hand to the left. The puppy should follow.

*Puppy receives reward*

*Puppy slows down*

## Problem Solving

### LOSING CONCENTRATION
If the puppy's attention wanders, put your left hand under its collar and bring it back to the correct heel position.

*Food scent lures distracted puppy*

### BOISTEROUS BEHAVIOUR
If the puppy does not respond to food lures, draw its attention to a favourite toy. Use a longline to ensure the puppy's compliance.

*Puppy notices toy*

*Owner calls puppy's name*

### JUMPING UP
To discourage jumping, hold the puppy's collar with your left hand and entice it with the hidden reward held low.

*Right hand crosses owner's body*

### ENJOYABLE TRAINING
If the puppy is not interested in one type of food reward, try another, or switch to a favourite squeaky toy. You should keep training sessions short, no more than a few minutes at a time, and always end them with a period of enjoyable play.

# Walking on a Lead

Your puppy's safety and well-being depend on you. A dog should never be allowed to run free, unless it is under your supervision in a protected environment, and away from danger. You should have already trained your puppy to sit and to lie down while wearing a lead *(see page 42)*, and to walk with you without wearing a lead *(see page 44)*. Now you can teach it to walk on the lead without pulling.

**1** Start training indoors. Let the puppy look at and smell the lead. Then attach the lead to the puppy's well-fitting, comfortable collar *(see page 32)*.

**2** With the puppy on your left side, hold the lead and a food reward in your right hand. Your left hand should also hold the slack lead. Command the puppy to sit.

*Left hand is ready to slide down lead to collar*

HEEL

*Lead is given a quick, light jerk*

**3** Begin to walk, setting off with your left foot. As the puppy walks beside you, give the command "Heel". If the puppy surges forwards, slide your left hand down to its collar and gently pull backwards.

"GOOD DOG"

**4** When the puppy is in the heel position, give the reward and say "Good dog". Then command the puppy to sit, and repeat "Good dog". Gradually increase the distance you cover as the puppy obeys the sequence of commands.

*Puppy maintains concentration*

"STEADY"

*Puppy is close to owner's leg*

"HEEL"

*Owner holds puppy back by its collar*

**5** Once the puppy is able to walk to heel and sit obediently as you go from room to room, you can train it to turn right. Guide the puppy around to the right with your left hand, and give the command "Heel".

**6** To make a left turn, increase your own speed and hold the food in front of the puppy's nose to slow it down. Keep the puppy close to your left leg, and give the command "Steady" as it slows down.

## Problem Solving

**CLIMBING UP THE LEAD**
If the puppy tries to jump up on you or climb the lead, sternly say "No" or "Off". Move away, command the puppy to sit, and go back to the beginning of the exercise. Do not train on outdoor walks at first, since these can be too distracting. Train indoors, then slowly graduate to busier locations.

**COLLAPSING**
If the puppy refuses to move, gently and patiently entice it with a favourite squeaky toy. Do not pull the puppy, or become angry. Encourage the puppy with praise, and allow it to build up its confidence.

**PULLING FORWARDS**
Command the puppy to sit each time it pulls. Neither you nor the puppy should lose concentration, and you should not shout the commands. Use a head halter on boisterous dogs.

# Suitable Toys

Puppies chew objects in order to learn about their environment, but chewing can be an expensive problem. By encouraging your dog to chew its own specific toys, you will prevent it from damaging other household items. Always choose safe toys, and limit their availability to prevent the dog from becoming possessive about them.

## TYPES OF TOY

BALL-ON-A-ROPE

ROPE

RAWHIDE BALL

RAWHIDE CHEW

RUBBER BONES

PLASTIC BONE

### Indestructible and delicious
The best dog toys have their own unique smells, and are unlike anything else a dog might find. Through trial and error, you will learn which toys your dog prefers. Balls are good for chasing, catching, and retrieving, while bones are satisfying to chew. Tug toys are ideal for a tug-of-war with your dog, or for two dogs to play with, but should only be used with gentle dogs (see page 79). Squeaky toys must be well made, since dogs tend to destroy them and could swallow the "squeaker".

RUBBER TOY

CHEW TOY

SOFT TOY BONE

HOLLOW BONE

THROW BALL

TUG TOY

STERILIZED BONE

RUBBER RING

CHEW STICKS

SQUEAKY MOUSE

COLOURED CHEW STICKS

# MAKING A CHEW TOY

**1** To make a satisfying chew toy for your dog, insert cheese spread into the core of a sterilized bone.

*Cheese spread is inserted deep into hollow*

**2** Give the bone to the dog, who will try to reach the food in the centre. You can help the dog reach the last morsel of cheese, deep in the bone. This is an ideal toy to stimulate a dog when it is at home alone.

*Dog enjoys challenge of bone*

**3** In sight of the dog, put the toy away. Dogs soon learn that toys belong to their owners and are given only on special occasions.

## Destructive Chewing

*Old shoes smell like new ones*

This dog is innocently chewing on its owner's personal items. Avoid giving a dog old clothes or shoes to play with. If dogs are allowed to chew these items, they will assume that they may chew any other articles of clothing. Dogs cannot distinguish between old items and new ones.

# TUG-OF-WAR

*Soft toy is robust*

*Dog anchors itself and pulls back*

These two dogs are pulling at the same toy. Dogs can be very possessive about toys, so if you have two dogs make sure that the toys are not too attractive to fight over.

# New Experiences

Enlist the help of friends and neighbours who can provide your puppy with as many varied experiences as possible. If you have your own garden, begin training in it as soon as possible. With your vet's approval, take your puppy to public places so that it becomes accustomed to traffic noise, pedestrians, car journeys and, most importantly, to obeying you in a variety of different environments and circumstances. Do not wait for problems to develop. Introduce your puppy to people in uniform, such as postmen, to children, and to other adults who look or dress differently from you.

## MEETING PEOPLE

**Frightening strangers**

A person with a beard, someone wearing a hat, or someone with a different skin complexion to the dog's human family can be intimidating. Enlisting the help of friends, set up meetings between them and the dog. Reward the dog when it shows curiosity but remains calm.

**A positive approach**

Instruct children to approach the dog quietly, and stroke it from the side. Reward the dog with verbal praise or a food treat when it behaves calmly.

*Man avoids intimidating eye contact with dog*

*Gentle stroking is accepted by dog*

*Hand is offered for investigation and scenting*

*An umbrella can appear threatening*

*Dog shows no signs of apprehension*

*Stroking under chin is not intimidating*

**Outdoor rendezvous**

Arrange for the dog to meet new people inside your home first, and then outdoors. This will prepare the dog for later meetings with people who will try to stroke it without asking your permission. Instruct your friends to sit on their haunches when greeting the puppy, so that they do not intimidate it. Ask a friend to offer a food treat, so that the puppy will learn to welcome approaches from other people.

# OUTDOOR TRAINING

### Road sense
Once the puppy responds to commands in your home and garden, you can move to busier environments. You should always command the dog to sit before crossing a road.

### Hand signals
Hand signals are very important outdoors, where you want the dog to obey even when it is far away from you. You should use dramatic gestures.

*Hand is held high so that dog does not miss signal*

## CAR JOURNEYS

*Lead ensures that owner is in control*

### Introducing the car
The back of a car can be a frightening place, especially if the dog's first experience in it causes motion sickness and nausea. Before actually driving anywhere, entice the dog into your parked car with a food reward. Once the dog is happy to sit in the car, accustom it to the sound of the engine. Train the dog to look upon the car as a second home *(see page 108)*.

*Dog willingly prepares to jump into car, following food reward*

### Reward quiet behaviour
Give food rewards and verbal praise when the dog displays no signs of agitation or nausea. Go for short drives initially, and gradually increase their duration. Always reward the dog for settling down and remaining quiet.

## Playing with Other Dogs
Although dogs must learn how to behave with humans, they should also be able to play with other dogs. By removing a puppy from its mother and littermates when it is eight weeks old, humans prevent the dog from learning naturally how to behave with its own kind. You can overcome this problem by arranging for the puppy to attend weekly supervised puppy classes *(see page 122)*. The puppy will learn what canine body language means, and how it can use body language when communicating with other dogs. This type of early experience reduces the risks of conflicts later in the dog's life.

*Puppy investigates new class member*

# CHAPTER THREE

# Further Training

O nce your dog has learned basic commands, you can train it to walk quietly with you, bark only under the correct circumstances, control the use of its paws, hold and retrieve objects, and behave properly with children and other animals. It is important to remember that some dogs are more difficult to train than others. Make training as simple as possible by ensuring that your pet has learned how to behave with other dogs and with people. It is essential that you use collars and leads correctly, and choose training equipment suitable for your dog's shape and temperament. Although it is easiest to train a puppy, it is still simple and only slightly more time consuming to obedience train an adult dog. The result will be a well-mannered and reliable canine companion.

# Control and Restraint

It is essential that you use an appropriate form of control when training your dog, and indeed when you are in any public place. Most dogs respond to the pull of a half-check collar, but others are more responsive to head halters or harnesses. Also, where laws or common sense dictate, make sure that your dog wears a muzzle *(see pages 33 and 77)*.

## HALF-CHECK COLLAR

1 Make sure you position your dog's half-check collar correctly; the soft webbing should be around its throat and the chain links should be over the top of its neck.

2 Pull upwards on the lead to tighten the collar. This controls unwanted activity in most dogs without causing discomfort. Avoid using check collars on dogs with delicate windpipes.

*Hook on lead is attached to collar ring*

*Fabric lies comfortably across delicate windpipe*

## BODY HARNESSES

**Emergency harness**
Loop the lead across the dog's chest and hold it close to its body. This enables you to retain firm control of the dog if it becomes frightened and pulls unexpectedly.

*Lead is threaded through handle*

**Standard harness**
With the harness correctly positioned, the dog is controlled by tension to the rib cage. A harness is suitable for breeds with soft windpipes, such as Yorkshire Terriers, and for those with muscular necks, such as Pugs.

*Harness fits securely around chest*

# HEAD HALTER

**1** Slip the head halter over the dog's muzzle, putting your hand under its jaw to hold its head up.

*Owner gives food reward*

**2** Fasten the halter behind the dog's neck, making sure that it is not too tight. You should be able to get two fingers under any part of the halter.

**3** The lead is attached to the halter ring under the dog's lower jaw. If the dog pulls forwards, its momentum pulls its head down and closes its jaws.

**4** By pulling your arm back to your side, you can bring the dog back to its correct heel position.

*Lead tension guides dog back into position*

*Halter tightens safely around muzzle*

## Muzzling a Dog

### POSITIONING A MUZZLE
Kneel to the side of the dog and position the muzzle from below the dog's head.

### FASTENING A MUZZLE
Once the muzzle is positioned correctly, pull the straps gently behind the dog's neck and fasten them. Make sure that the muzzle fits securely, but that it is not too tight. The dog should be able to open its jaws and pant freely while wearing the muzzle.

*Straps are adjustable*

### FIRST-TIME USE
The dog may try to take off the muzzle at first. You should never attempt to remove the muzzle while the dog is pawing at it. Instead, distract the dog and remove the muzzle when it has quietened down. Muzzled dogs should not be left unsupervised for long periods of time. Muzzling not only prevents the dog from scavenging and minimizes the risk of bites, but also reminds it that you are in control.

# Sit and Stay

The commands "Sit" and "Stay" form the basis of responsible pet ownership and are useful forms of control during outdoor activity. Begin training in a quiet indoor area such as a hallway, and limit each session to 15 minutes. Once your dog has learned to respond consistently to your word commands, you may use simple hand signals *(see page 62).*

1 With the dog on your left side, hold the telescoped lead at waist level in your left hand, and a food reward in your right. As the dog sits, in order to concentrate on the treat, give the command "Sit" *(see page 42).*

"STAY"

2 Maintaining tension on the lead, step forwards with your right foot. Give the command "Stay" as you move forwards.

*Body turns towards dog*

*Food treat is palmed but obvious*

*Dog looks up intently*

3 Maintaining eye contact with the dog, move your left foot to join your right foot.

4 Exerting light pressure on the lead and holding it over the dog's head, turn to face the dog. Keep its concentration by holding the food reward high above its head.

*Feet do not move and there are no signs of jumping up*

5 Reward the dog for staying. Now slowly walk around the dog, holding the lead above its head. Issue as few commands as possible, so that you do not confuse the dog.

*Dog senses contact through taut lead*

*Dog obediently remains still*

6 After several sessions, the dog should sit and stay while on the lead. Now drop the lead and repeat each of the five previous steps, always praising the dog for good behaviour.

*Owner keeps her hands by her sides*

*Dog concentrates on owner, waiting for command or reward*

7 When the dog obediently sits and stays with the lead dropped, give it the reward. It is important to give rewards while the dog is doing what you command, not after it has moved.

"GOOD DOG"

*Food reward is held up to maintain eye contact*

8 After you have rewarded the dog, release it from the training session by opening your arms and saying "OK".

"OK"

### If the Dog Moves

You are teaching the dog a completely new language, so do not expect it to understand the commands immediately. If the dog moves, or if it does not naturally sit and stay in order to observe its potential food reward, hold it by the collar with your left hand and tuck its bottom down with your right.

*Left hand holds head up*

*Right hand tucks dog's bottom under*

# Come and Sit

You will often notice potential dangers before your dog does, so teaching it to return to you on command is essential for its safety. As a puppy your dog comes to you for security, but as an adult it should be trained to return because it wants to be with you. Recall training is rewarding and fun, and the best results are obtained when a reliable bond has been established between you and your canine companion.

**1** The dog should have previously learned to sit and stay (see page 56). With the lead in your left hand and a food treat in your right, walk away giving the command "Stay".

*Lead is telescoped in left hand*

*Eye contact between dog and owner is maintained*

*Food is held close to body*

**2** Turn to face the dog, holding it on the lead, and show it the food reward. Call the dog, using its name and the command "Come".

**3** As the dog reaches you, give the command "Sit". Many dogs will naturally sit in order to keep an eye on the reward, but you should still issue the command as the dog sits down.

**4** Once the dog has learned to return to you on a standard lead, progress to a longline. A toy reward will be most visible to the dog from a distance.

*Owner waves toy*

*Longline is slack but ensures compliance with command*

"PRINCE COME"

"GOOD DOG"

"SIT"

6 With the dog's lead over your shoulder and the toy in your pocket, call the dog and command it to sit. Proceed to this stage once the dog reliably comes to you on the longline.

*Reward is visible to dog*

*Dog sits on hearing command*

*Tug toys are ideal rewards for dogs that enjoy mouthing objects*

5 When the dog obediently responds to the "Come" and "Sit" commands, give it the toy reward and praise it.

*Dog sits obediently before receiving reward*

## Extra Information

### HAVE PATIENCE
The "Sit", "Stay", and "Come" commands are the most important lessons you can teach a dog, since they enable you to keep it under control at all times. All dog owners have a responsibility for ensuring that their pets are not a nuisance. Praise the dog when it responds well and always use a positive tone of voice. When it does not obey a command, repeat the exercise from the previous level of success.

### HAVE FUN
Training should be fun for both you and the dog. Use rewards freely at first, and soon the dog will come to you because it enjoys your company. Always finish training sessions with games or play, so that the dog will look forward to the next lesson. Be theatrical during exercises that involve moving around, because dogs enjoy this.

# Lie Down

Training your dog to lie down reliably on your command is a valuable lesson, especially during outdoor activity where there are dangers such as busy roads. Your dog will also learn that you are in control, which is particularly important if it is a dominant and assertive individual. There are two lying down positions: "sphinx", in which the hind legs are tucked under, and "flat", where the hips are rolled and the legs are to one side.

*Fingers are under collar*

**1** With the dog on the lead on your left side, command it to sit *(see page 42)*. Kneel down and tuck the lead under your knees. Hold the dog's collar with your left hand, and hold a food reward in your right palm.

*Dog concentrates on food reward*

*Lead is secured under knees*

**2** With the food hidden in your closed fist, let the dog smell the scent. This focuses the dog's mind, while your hand under the collar prevents the dog from moving forwards.

*Owner controls movement by holding collar*

*Hand makes an L-shape*

**3** Move your right hand straight down, then forwards between the dog's forepaws. As the dog drops to follow the food, give the command "Down".

**4** As soon as the dog lies down, give the food reward. At this stage, it does not matter which position the dog assumes, as long as it is comfortable.

*Dog begins to assume relaxed position*

# EMERGENCY ACTION

To put the dog into the instant down position, bend your knees, slide your hand down the lead to the collar, and pull down, locking your wrist and elbow. Issue the command "Down". Reward the dog with praise when it is in the down position. Training the dog to lie down indoors, or in a quiet garden where there are few distractions, is easier than training in more stimulating surroundings. Once the dog has mastered the lesson in a relatively quiet place, you will be able to move to a more stimulating environment.

*Owner gives authoritative command*

*Dog is guided down firmly and quickly*

*Head goes down first*

## Problem Solving

"DOWN"

*Owner pulls downwards on collar*

### REINFORCING THE DOWN
If the dog's shoulders rise from the down position before it has been released, run your hand firmly down the lead to the collar. This controls the upwards movement, and exerts pressure downwards. As the dog goes back down, repeat the command "Down" The dog should only leave the down position when you say "OK".

### RELUCTANT DOGS
If the dog is not food oriented, try changing the reward. Use a chew toy that the dog is obsessed with *(see page 94)*. Only physically assist dogs into the down position *(see page 43)* if they accept being touched. If you have a dominant dog, only use rewards. If these methods fail, enlist professional help.

### AVOIDING INJURY
Do not apply pressure over delicate areas such as the kidney, rib cage, bladder, and liver regions.

*Kidneys*    *Rib cage*

*Liver*

*Bladder*

# Down and Stay

Jumping up on people and chasing are part of natural dog behaviour, but they can be unpleasant and even dangerous activities. By teaching your dog to stay down on command you can control these unwanted actions. Use verbal commands and rewards, but also use simple hand signals so that your dog can understand your commands from a distance.

"STAY"

**1** With the dog on your left side in the down position *(see page 60)*, give the command "Stay" *(see page 56)*. Holding the lead in your right hand, move your left hand down towards the dog, and walk away.

*Palm towards dog signals "Stay"*

*Dog watches hand signal*

**2** Maintain eye contact with the dog, and hold the lead loosely as you walk away. Do not use a food reward when training the dog to stay down, since it will want to come to you for it.

*Lead ensures control*

*Owner observes dog by using mirror*

"GOOD DOG"

**3** Still maintaining eye contact, turn, stand still, and repeat "Stay". Reward the dog by saying "Good dog". Gradually extend the duration of the down position until the dog stays down for several minutes.

**4** Having been trained to remain in the down position in your presence, the dog can be trained to stay down in your absence. Repeat the first three steps, and then leave the room. Using a mirror to look around the door, make sure that the dog does not move.

*Dog cannot see owner*

**5** After a few minutes, return to the dog and give the verbal reward "Good dog". You should reward the dog calmly and quietly when it is still lying down. Do not excite the dog, and do not reward it for getting up.

"GOOD DOG"

**6** Release the dog from the down position with the word "OK". Do not excite the dog by being too flamboyant, because excitement is such a good reward that the dog will only look forward to the end of the exercise, and not to the training itself.

*Dog rises up eagerly*

*Open palm signals release*

## PROBLEM SOLVING

### DISOBEYING COMMANDS
If the dog moves while you are observing it through the mirror, go back in to the room and move around in the dog's sight while it is still in the down position.

### DISTRACTING THE DOG
To prepare for training the dog in distracting environments, make loud noises while you are watching it through the mirror. As the dog starts to move, go back into the room and repeat the command "Down". Do not rush towards the dog or display anger, since this will cause it to be excited.

## PRACTICAL USES

You should train the dog to remain lying down even when unexpected activity occurs. This ensures safety for the dog and for other people, while displaying its obedient behaviour.

*Dog lies completely relaxed*

# Prolonged Lie Down

The results of training your dog to lie down on command for an extended period of time will be satisfying for both you and your pet. You will be able to take your dog on shopping trips, or even to your workplace, fully confident that when you tell it to lie down it will be in the same position 20 minutes later. This exercise requires patient training, but it is worth the extra time and effort to have a reliable canine companion.

**1** Position the dog beside your chair and give the command "Down-stay" *(see page 62).* Hold the dog's lead loosely.

*Owner monitors dog*

**2** As the dog begins to move, hold it by the collar and pull it gently back into position. Say "No" and repeat the command "Down-stay".

*Dog is distracted by activities, odours, or noises*

*Owner issues command before leg straightens*

**3** If, after several minutes, the dog attempts to leave the down position again, you should intervene immediately. Say "No" as the dog rises, and give the command "Down-stay" as you reinforce the down position.

*Dog is relaxed but alert*

*Dog instantly obeys command*

*Body returns to the "sphinx" position*

4 After a while, the dog should assume a more comfortable resting position on its side. Whereas it is easy for the dog to instantly leave the "sphinx" position *(see page 60)*, once it lies on its side it has accepted your command for a prolonged down.

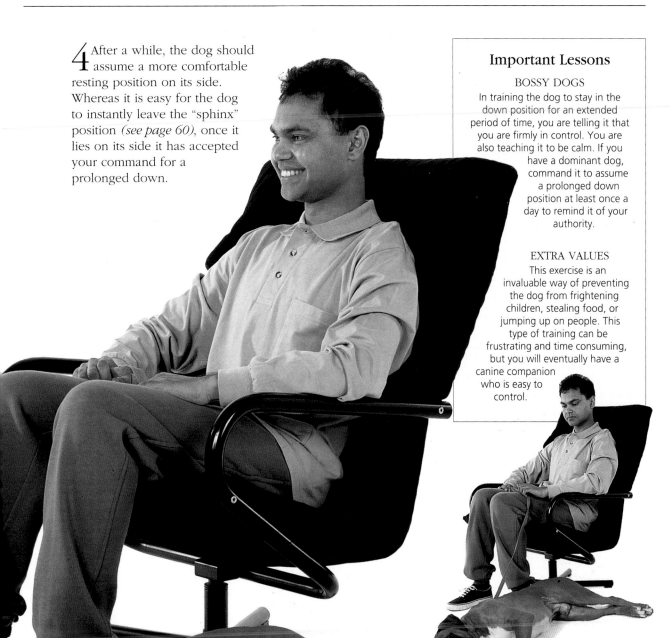

### Important Lessons

BOSSY DOGS
In training the dog to stay in the down position for an extended period of time, you are telling it that you are firmly in control. You are also teaching it to be calm. If you have a dominant dog, command it to assume a prolonged down position at least once a day to remind it of your authority.

EXTRA VALUES
This exercise is an invaluable way of preventing the dog from frightening children, stealing food, or jumping up on people. This type of training can be frustrating and time consuming, but you will eventually have a canine companion who is easy to control.

5 Twenty minutes later the dog should still be in a fully relaxed position. Increase the duration of this exercise gradually over several training sessions, until the dog is completely reliable.

# Bark Control

Abarking dog offers protection and makes an excellent burglar alarm, but you do need an on-off switch. When your dog has learned to "speak" on command you will be able not only to control its barking, but also to command it to be quiet. Once the dog knows that barking is only permitted under specific circumstances, it can be trained to bark on command, or on hearing such sounds as smoke alarms or noises outside a window. You should initially train to rewards like food and toys, then add verbal praise.

1 Attach the dog's lead to a fence or post, and stand about 1 metre (3 ft) away. Tease the dog by showing it a toy, and give a food reward when it barks with frustration.

*Food is ready to be given at moment of barking*

*Alert dog concentrates on activity*

2 Put the toy away, and change the reward from a food treat to a verbal "Good dog" when the dog barks, but give a more gratifying food treat occasionally.

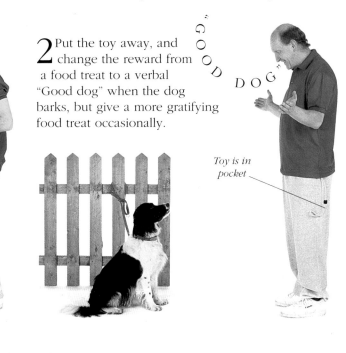

*"GOOD DOG"*

*Toy is in pocket*

3 Give the command "Speak" the moment the dog barks, then give the toy as a reward. Correct timing is essential here, and by observing the dog's body language you can anticipate the bark *(see page 22).*

*"SPEAK"*

*Barking dog is rewarded with toy*

4 Once the dog understands the command "Speak", give the command "Quiet" when the dog is barking. Give the toy reward as soon as the dog stops barking, but put the toy away and command "No" if it continues.

*"NO"*

*Owner does not give reward to barking dog*

**5** After teaching the dog to bark or be quiet when you are near, move a short distance away from it. Patiently repeat the exercise from the beginning, until the dog learns to respond to the commands.

*"SPEAK"*

*Owner anticipates bark and times his command*

*Potential reward is visible to dog*

**6** Return to the dog and reward it with its favourite toy. Continue repeating the exercise until the dog consistently responds to intermittent rewards while secured to the fence. Then release the dog and continue training with it off the lead.

*Dog is rewarded by being allowed to chew toy*

*Dog has not moved*

## Useful Variations

ALTERNATIVE "QUIET"
If the dog is food oriented, try putting a tasty morsel of food on its nose to stop it from barking. Timing your command perfectly, say "Quiet" as the dog stops barking, then give the food treat. Only reward the dog when it is silent.

*"QUIET"*

*Dog cannot sniff and bark simultaneously*

*Owner senses danger*

*"GUARD"*

*Dog barks on command*

PROTECTION
Most people only require their dog to bark as a means of defence, so teaching the command "Guard" rather than "Speak" is a useful option. A barking dog is a good deterrent against intruders in the home, or against potential attackers outdoors.

# Learning to Touch

Training a dog to use its paw teaches it dexterity, and some dogs are more adept at this than others. It is a way in which dogs can communicate, and is also the basis for "shaking hands" – a valuable game, since raising a paw is a subservient gesture. By training your dog to carry out this exercise, you are reinforcing your pack-leader status.

**1** With the dog on your left side, command it to sit. Kneeling down, hold the dog's collar in your left hand, and show it the food you have concealed in your right hand.

*Dog concentrates on potential treat*

**2** Move your right hand down to the floor, until it is in front of the dog's paws. Hold the collar to prevent the dog from lying down.

*Dog is restrained from putting muzzle near food reward*

**3** Push the treat towards the dog's paws. As the dog lifts its paw, move your clenched hand under it, and then slightly up off the floor. Continue to restrain the dog by the collar.

*Paw makes contact with owner's hand*

**4** With the dog's paw resting on your fist, lift it up and give the command "Paw". Then give the food reward. Repeat the exercise, using "Paw" to reward the response, instead of food.

"PAW"

**5** Once the dog consistently raises its paw to your hand on verbal command alone, show it that you are concealing a food reward behind a small piece of plywood.

*Food snack is hidden from view*

## Excessive Pawing

If the dog demands attention by pawing at you excessively, say "No" firmly and command it to lie down. Be aware, however, that the dog is letting you know that it needs mental and physical stimulation.

*Owner uses stern tone of voice*

*"NO"*

*Contact is used to seek attention*

*Dog exercises reflexes, and catches object in mid-air*

**6** Give the command "Paw", and reward the dog with the food treat when it touches the plywood. This is the basis for a variety of touch games.

## TOUCH GAME

Once the dog has learned how to use its paw on command, it can be trained to open doors and play mentally stimulating games. Touching a panel on this box ejects an object for the dog to catch.

*Touching panel with paw releases toy*

# Walking to Heel

It is useful if your dog knows how to sit obediently *(see page 56)* before you train it to walk to heel. Start training in a quiet room, walking towards a door that does not lead outdoors. Gradually increase distractions until the dog walks to heel out of the front door without becoming overexcited. If your dog is powerful or boisterous, using a head halter will give you the best control *(see page 55)*. Avoid constantly repeating the "Heel" command.

**1** Start training with the dog in the sit position on your left side. Hold the telescoped lead and a food reward in your right hand, and hold the other end of the lead close to the dog's collar with your left hand.

**2** Using the dog's name and the command "Heel", begin to walk, leading with your left foot. Keep the dog close to your left thigh. Give the food reward when the dog has walked to heel for a few paces.

*"SHEP HEEL"*

*"SHEP HEEL"*

*Dog follows food reward*

*Lead is slack*

*Lead is held in both hands*

**3** When the dog is able to walk 20 paces without restraint, use a food reward as an inducement to turn right.

*Light jerks on lead will bring dog back into position*

**4** Sliding your hand down the lead to the dog's collar, and leading with your left leg, increase your speed while slowing down the dog for a left turn.

*"SHEP HEEL"*

*"HEEL"*

*Dog is still close to owner's thigh*

**5** You can now make an about turn. Still using food to lure the dog, say the dog's name and give the command "Heel", while turning a full circle.

*Dog listens to command*

## Heeling off the Lead

**1** When the dog has been trained to walk to heel on the lead, repeat the exercise without the lead. Put the lead over your shoulder and hold a food reward in your right hand.

*Raised tail shows that dog is happy to obey*

*"HEEL"*

**2** Keeping the dog close to your left leg, and holding the food reward in your right hand, give the command "Heel" and draw the dog to the right.

*"HEEL"*

*Dog follows food reward closely*

**3** Reaching across the front of your body, with the food in your right hand, set off with your left foot to make a left turn. Give the command "Heel" as you do so. The dog will slow down in order to stay near to the food.

*"HEEL"*

*Owner moves faster than dog*

# Holding Objects

One of the most enjoyable games that you can play with your dog involves fetching objects *(see page 74)*. However, first the dog must learn to hold an object in its mouth. Do not use squeaky toys in this exercise, since your dog will want to chew them. Use a small piece of rolled-up carpet or a special retrieve dummy. You should only reward with verbal and physical praise – not food treats – since the dog must continue to hold the object.

## HOLDING AN OBJECT

1 Kneel beside the dog, who should be sitting. Hold the lead under your knees and your left arm around the dog's head. Gently open the dog's mouth, saying "Good dog".

*Fingers feel jaw tension*

*"HOLD"*

*Jaw is opened gently with thumb*

2 Having previously teased the dog with the training object, and after you have made sure that it is not unhappy, hold the dog's head up and put the object into its mouth. Now give the command "Hold".

3 The dog should hold the object willingly and correctly just behind its canine teeth, with its tongue retracted. Praise the dog by saying "Good dog to hold".

*"GOOD DOG TO HOLD"*

*Object is gripped comfortably*

# PICKING UP AN OBJECT

**1** Now you can teach the dog to pick up the object. Tease the dog by bringing the object up to its nose.

*"GOOD DOG"*

*Dog concentrates on object*

*Dog can smell and see object*

*Owner kneels on lead*

**2** Move the object down towards the floor. The dog should be interested and should follow the object intently. Give the verbal reward "Good dog".

**3** Rest the object on the floor, but do not take your hand away. Command "Hold" as the dog moves forwards to take the object in its mouth.

*"HOLD"*

*"HOLD"*

**4** Remove your hand from the object, and the dog should pick it up. At the same moment, repeat the command "Hold", ensuring that the dog does not drop the object.

## Problem Solving

*"BAH"*

*Object is reinserted*

*Dog is held in position*

### REJECTING THE OBJECT
If the dog attempts to spit out the object, say "Bah!" and hold it in place. Do not say "Hold" at this stage, or the dog will associate that word with an experience of holding that it does not enjoy. Go back to the beginning of the exercise.

### AVOIDING THE OBJECT
If the dog turns its head away from the object, follow the dog's head and always keep the object at nose level.

*Object is kept close to dog's nose*

*Object does not sit behind canine teeth*

*Tongue has difficulty retracting*

### DIFFICULT HOLDS
Some dogs, such as Boxers, have overshot jaws, so they must hold objects in front of, rather than behind, their canine teeth.

# Retrieving Objects

Once your dog has learned to hold and pick up an object, it is ready to learn to chase it and bring it back to you. If you are training a puppy, use a squeaky toy initially and let the puppy play with it. Otherwise, use the same object that you used in the previous exercise *(see page 72)*. These exercises offer your dog mental and physical stimulation.

**1** With the dog's lead attached for guaranteed control, hold the dog by its collar with one hand as you throw the object a short distance.

*Dog watches object*

**2** Give the command "Fetch" as you release your hold on the dog's collar. Having been trained to pick up and hold the object, the dog should now chase it.

"FETCH"

*Dog on lead is under owner's control*

"COME"

**3** Once the dog has picked up the object, give the command "Come" to recall it. Crouch down to encourage the dog, and give gentle jerks on the lead if necessary.

*Dog grips object firmly*

**4** Reward the dog for its obedience with firm strokes down its side and the verbal praise "Good dog". Put your hand under the dog's jaw to prevent it from dropping the object.

*"GOOD DOG"*

*Dog remains standing*

**5** Issue the command "Give", and take the object from the dog's mouth. As soon as the dog releases the object, reward it with the words "Good dog".

*"GIVE"*

*Dog relinquishes object*

**6** Reminding the dog that you are still in control, command it to sit. Give the object back to the dog as a final reward.

## Problem Solving

### RELUCTANT TO FETCH
If the dog is unwilling to fetch the object, make the game more interesting by using a squeaky toy and running with the dog on its lead to where you have thrown the object. Gradually increase the distance that you throw the toy.

### RELUCTANT TO HOLD
If the dog runs to the object but then appears to be puzzled, it has not learned to hold properly. Teach the "Hold" command again *(see page 72)*, using a more interesting toy.

### RELUCTANT TO RETURN
If the dog picks up the object but does not respond to your command to come, go back to recall training *(see page 58)* before continuing the retrieve exercise.

### DROPPING THE OBJECT
A dog that picks up the thrown object, and starts carrying it back but then drops it, needs more lessons in holding *(see page 72)*. When the dog is proficient in this exercise, continue with the retrieve routine, starting with short distances and gradually increasing them.

### PUPPY RETRIEVING
You can turn this exercise into a game to play with a puppy. Let the puppy chew the toy, and do not try to take it away. Praise the puppy when it naturally drops the object. Puppies usually take their toys to a "safe place", so you should begin by throwing the object from there.

*Arms held wide to attract puppy*

*Toy feels exciting to carry*

# Dogs and Children

It is just as important to train children how to approach dogs as it is to train dogs how to behave with children. You should teach your children that not all dogs are friendly, and that they should always ask the owner's permission before touching a dog. Instruct them never to rush up to a dog, or to tease it or shout at it. Children should not be given responsibility for training or feeding a dog until they are mature and sensible.

### No eye contact
You should ensure that children make eye contact with you rather than the dog. Because children are smaller and less authoritative than adults, they are more at risk from bites.

*Boy looks at owner and asks to stroke dog*

### Gentle strokes
Instruct children to stroke the dog from the side, not from the front, and tell them that they should never pat the dog's head. Praise the dog for its good behaviour, but be prepared to reprimand it if it snaps or growls through fear.

*Boy gives long strokes along dog's side*

### Excitement and obedience
Train the dog to lie down, even in the presence of exciting activity such as children playing with a ball. Dogs naturally nip and chew in a playful context, so do not leave them alone with small children.

*Dog is alert but relaxed in presence of children*

## Canine manners

Teach the dog not to grab food from children by training it to take food only when permitted *(see page 121)*. Reward the dog for sitting obediently while a child eats.

## Adult responsibilities

Only adult members of the family should feed the dog. Do not let children carry food near the dog.

## Introductions to infants

Allow a new dog to scent and investigate a child only if you are sure the dog is reliable, and only in your presence.

*This dog is not frightened by children*

## Safety first

A dog should wear a muzzle in the presence of toddlers. This is particularly important if the dog guards or chases, if it has ever threatened or bitten anyone, or if it has not been well trained in obedience.

### Meeting the New Baby

*Dog is interested in baby*

*Baby is present when dog is fed*

Allow the dog to see and smell, but not to touch, a new baby. You should praise, play with, and feed the dog in the baby's presence. An infant's squeals and jerky movements can stimulate nervous behaviour, and if you are worried you should seek professional help.

# Games with Dogs

Dogs thrive on both mental and physical stimulation. They are also inquisitive, and enjoy human companionship. By playing constructive games with your dog, you can alleviate boredom, channel its natural jumping behaviour, and reduce any destructive activity. By controlling the games, you will reinforce your authority over the dog.

### Frisbee games
Catching a Frisbee and returning it is an exciting game for active, healthy dogs, but can be physically demanding, and even dangerous, for elderly or overweight animals.

*Arms are held open to welcome dog*

*Use purpose-made toys with rounded edges*

*Dog jumps to catch ball*

### Playing with balls
Catch and drop is a simple game that tests the dog's reactions and obedience. Always throw the ball away from the dog, not towards it. Throwing a ball towards a dog is dangerous, since it could go down the dog's throat when it is caught.

### Activity games
Train the dog to participate in purpose-made activity games. Many dog clubs hold competitions involving these games, and it is enjoyable for both you and the dog to participate in them.

*"Flying mouse" is ejected from box when dog touches lever*

### Hide-and-seek
Playing hide-and-seek with the dog tests its mental and scenting abilities. Alternatively, train the dog to seek out hidden objects like a set of keys, a wallet, a shoe, or a slipper – but only on your command.

*Owner hides behind door*

*Toy is designed for retrieving, chewing, and tug-of-war*

### Tug-of-war
Only play tug-of-war when the dog learns to drop an object on command *(see page 75)*, and always use specially made, robust toys. Never play "mouthing" games with possessive dogs, since they might react aggressively.

### Jogging
Healthy dogs need plenty of exercise, and training the dog to run to heel with you while you jog is both enjoyable and physically stimulating.

### Following a scent
Many dogs, especially scent hounds, enjoy the mental concentration of following a scent trail. You can lay down a track for the dog by walking through grass, leaving a reward at the end.

## Additional Information
### USING TOYS
When you have finished playing with the dog, make a point of putting the toys away, preferably in their own bag or box. The dog will soon learn that the toys belong to you, and that it is only allowed to play with them under your terms. This makes the toys more desirable, so that you can use them as potent rewards during or after training. They are also useful as play objects when the dog is left at home alone.

### REWARDING GAMES
Playing games can be rewarding for both you and the dog. If possible, play games after each training session. You should avoid playing before training, since the dog will then be too tired to concentrate properly. You can incorporate training into your games by reinforcing the "Come", "Sit", "Stay", "Down", and "Drop" commands throughout, and by using play as the reward. If family members and friends participate in the games, the dog will receive rewards from a variety of people, and will learn to enjoy the companionship of all humans.

# Playing with Others

Most dogs enjoy playing with other canines if they had the opportunity to do so when they were young. Females will usually play more readily than males, who are more territorial, and more prone to fighting. Initial meetings between dogs should take place on neutral territory. Do not let your dog pull on its lead, since this stimulates aggression.

*Body language shows dog is relaxed*

### Meeting on neutral territory
Arrange for your dog to meet other dogs, with each dog on a lead. Let them investigate each other, but watch for aggressive eye contact. At the first sign of aggression, turn your dog's head away and produce a favourite toy as a distraction.

### Meeting through the fence
Once the dogs have successfully been introduced elsewhere, let them meet through a garden fence, or in front of your homes. Reward your dog's calm behaviour.

*Owner holds cat gently*

*Both dogs are on home territory*

*Clear hand signals are used*

### Meeting cats
First meetings between a dog and a cat should be supervised. Prevent the cat from running away, to avoid the dog chasing it.

### Responding to commands
Control the dog with verbal and physical commands when it is playing with other dogs. When you are ready to leave, use hand signals and verbal commands to instruct the dog to sit, then go to it and attach the lead.

*Dog sits obediently*

## Conflicts over possessions

Avoid conflicts over bones and other desirable items by either not giving them, or giving them in separate rooms. Many dogs naturally want what another dog has, even if they have an identical object, and bones and chews are the items most dogs fight over.

*Dog is content for the moment*

*Male asserts authority by standing over female*

## The opposite sex

Fighting is less likely between dogs of different sexes than it is between dogs of the same sex, and of similar ages and sizes. Initial meetings should take place with both dogs on their leads.

*Female behaves in subservient manner*

*Dog is alert but shows no sign of aggression*

## The same sex

Take care when dogs of the same size and sex meet. Do not permit lead tension, since this can provoke aggression. Reward the dog with verbal praise for quietly sniffing and investigating.

### New Dog in the Home

*Both dogs are on leads*

A new dog is a potential threat to the territory of the resident dog. Do not let a new puppy jump on the older dog, since the resident dog will find this unpleasant and provocative. Arrange meetings when both dogs are quiet and relaxed, and reward the dog for its obedience in the presence of the newcomer. Feed both dogs in the same room, making sure that there is no eye contact between them. Provide each dog with its own bed, placed in a private area. Continue to greet and reward the resident dog first, and try not to change your routines.

# CHAPTER FOUR

# *Overcoming Bad Habits*

Dogs are not perfect, and even the gentlest and
most obedient pet can develop unwanted
habits. If your dog develops bad habits, always try
to find and eliminate the cause – even though
avoiding a problem is often the easiest solution,
and is usually simpler than retraining the dog.
Dogs that destroy homes when they are left alone
do so not for reasons of revenge, but because they
are bored, frustrated, or suffering from separation
anxiety. Some bad habits, such as chasing
livestock or aggression towards other dogs, are
part of normal dog behaviour. This
makes them difficult to overcome, but slow,
repetitive, and consistent retraining is usually
effective. However, you should seek professional
help for the most dangerous or worrying
problems, such as fear biting or aggression
towards people.

# Understanding and Prevention

In order to correct your dog's bad habits, it is important to understand how they first developed. Although you may find your dog's behaviour unacceptable, to the dog it is a natural way to behave. When a problem develops, you should try to work out the reason for it. Ask yourself why the behaviour is unacceptable, and whether the dog understands that you regard it as wrong. Try to ascertain whether the behaviour can be prevented, redirected, or changed – either by yourself or by a trainer.

### Acceptable natural behaviour

Chewing bones, or toys that look like bones, is normal canine behaviour. Chewing is a way for dogs to find out about their environment.

*Object is held firmly by forepaws*

### Unacceptable natural behaviour

Chewing a shoe covered in human scent is a natural way for a dog to behave, but it is usually unacceptable to humans. You can prevent this bad habit from forming by never giving the dog old shoes to chew. The dog will learn to restrict its chewing to allowable objects.

*Hand is seen as potentially dangerous*

### Learned behaviour

Fear of hands is learned behaviour, and may occur if the dog has been abused at some time. You should prevent hand shyness by never using your hands to discipline the dog.

### Chewing for satisfaction

Many dogs delight in chewing objects, shredding newspaper, and even peeling wallpaper from walls. This desire to be "creative" requires acceptable outlets, such as bones to chew.

*Safe toys should either be digestible or indestructible*

*Dog looks content after satisfying its desire to chew*

### Destructive behaviour

Although destructive behaviour is satisfying to dogs, it is unacceptable to humans. Giving the dog too many toys teaches it to destroy other items. Limit the toys that you make available to the dog to three or four that are different from other household articles.

# BASIC CORRECTION TECHNIQUES

*Dog recognizes that raised finger means "No"*

### Discipline

It is important that the dog understands what kinds of behaviour you find unacceptable. You should only discipline the dog when it is actively misbehaving. Use a stern tone of voice when reprimanding the dog.

### Prevention

It is always easier to prevent problems than to cure them. Apply bitter spray to objects that are attractive to dogs, such as shoes *(see page 31)*.

*Spray is bitter, but non-toxic*

*Shoe will taste unpleasant to dog*

## Retraining Rules

Although bad habits vary, almost all of them can be corrected by following a standard retraining programme.

1 Make sure that the dog does something for you, such as sitting or lying down *(see pages 56 and 60)* before it receives verbal or physical rewards.
2 Go back to basic obedience training. Make sure that the dog sits and stays on command *(see page 56)*.
3 Ensure that the dog is always under your control. Both indoors and outdoors, keep the dog on a lead or longline until you are certain that it will respond to your commands.
4 Eliminate the satisfaction that the dog obtains from its bad behaviour. Sometimes this will involve mild punishment *(see page 21)*.
5 Persevere with the programme, and bear in mind that bad habits cannot be eliminated overnight. It may take several weeks before the problem is firmly under control.
6 For serious problems, in which injury to you, the dog, or other people is possible, you should seek professional help from a qualified dog trainer.

### Confinement

If the dog chews persistently, train it to stay in a crate when it is at home alone *(see page 34)*. Always provide the dog with acceptable toys to chew when it is in its crate.

*Toys provide an outlet for dog's natural behaviour*

# Assessing Temperament

It is an unfortunate fact that dog shelters experience a high rate of return. This is because many people make choices based on a dog's appearance, not its temperament. Rescued dogs are particularly prone to separation-related problems. If you are acquiring a dog that is more than six months old, you can test it for behavioural problems by carrying out a few exercises. Only take on a dog with such problems if you have the amount of time and patience that is required to deal with them.

## Nervousness

With the handler from the shelter holding the dog on a slack lead, quietly approach it from the front, maintaining eye contact. A relaxed dog will enjoy your approach, while a nervous dog may bark or cower.

*Dog is happy with direct eye contact*

## Hand shyness

With the dog still on a loose lead, stroke it under its chin, and then down its back. Talk to the dog quietly as you do this. A dog that fears hands will pull away.

*Dog willingly accepts being touched*

## Willingness to obey

Taking the lead from the handler, command the dog to sit. The dog's response will tell you whether it has had any obedience training.

## Willingness to respond

If the dog does not obey, tuck it into a sit position, in order to gauge its inclination to respond to training.

## Canine aggression

With the help of the handler, introduce the dog to a confident dog of the same sex. If the dog simply sniffs curiously there should be no problems with aggression towards other dogs.

### Fear of children

Holding the dog on a slack lead, introduce it to a child. The child should avoid direct eye contact with the dog. The response elicited will indicate whether the dog is nervous of children.

*Dog looks anxious, but remains quiet*

### Separation anxiety

Ascertain whether the dog barks, or shows any other signs of anxiety, when it is left alone in a room for ten minutes.

### Fear of strangers

Maintaining control with a slack lead, have the dog examined by a stranger. This will indicate any problems that might appear on visits to the vet or during grooming sessions.

*Dog shows no fear*

### Possessiveness

Holding the dog by its lead, remove its food bowl. Praise the dog, then return the food. If the dog shows no aggression, it is not likely to be possessive over food. Repeat this procedure using a toy and a bone.

*Lead is taut for control*

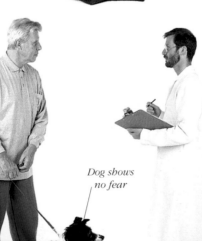

# Pulling on the Lead

Pulling on the lead is the most common problem experienced by dog owners. It can be caused by boredom or excitement, or it may be a manifestation of dominant behaviour. You should not attempt to match your strength against the dog's by repeatedly pulling back on the lead. If your pet pulls persistently, retrain it in basic obedience commands *(see pages 56–61)* and walking to heel *(see page 70)*, and follow the remedial techniques shown here. A head halter *(see page 55)* is useful on a large dog.

## THE PROBLEM

Sometimes the lead itself incites the dog to pull. It is therefore important not to use the lead as an object of force. You should try and assess why the dog pulls before attempting to correct its behaviour.

## THE REMEDY

1 Begin to walk with the dog on your left side, holding the lead in both hands. When the dog pulls, slide your left hand down the lead and pull back firmly.

*Hand pulls back once, gently but firmly*

2 When the dog is in the correct heel position, command it to sit. Start to walk again, giving the command "Heel". Repeat the procedure each time the dog pulls forwards.

3 Once the dog walks quietly to heel without pulling, reward it with a food treat. Gradually increase the distance you travel, but not the time of the training sessions.

*Owner gives food reward*

## OTHER REMEDIES

### "WAIT"

**Turning away**
When the dog pulls, use an element of surprise – turn immediately in the opposite direction. Praise the dog when it follows you.

*Lead is kept short*

### "WAIT"

**Hand signals**
As the dog lunges forwards, give the command "Wait", and put your right hand in front of its nose. Keep a firm grip on the lead with your left hand.

**No hand resistance**
Keeping the lead attached to the collar, loop it around your waist. Hold the lead lightly, and keep the dog in the heel position using food, a toy, or verbal commands as incentives.

*Titbit keeps dog's attention*

**Lead as harness**
To guarantee a short lead, and to reduce tension on the dog's neck, use its lead as a harness when bringing it back to the heel position *(see page 54).*

### Other Lead Problems

#### CHEWING AND CLIMBING
To young and boisterous dogs, leads are exciting new toys. Such dogs sometimes chew their leads, or try to climb them.

*Dog chews playfully*

#### THE REMEDY

Make the lead unpleasant to chew by spraying it with a bitter-tasting liquid *(see page 31).* When the dog tries to chew or climb the lead, it is disciplined by the unpleasant taste, rather than by you.

*Direct spray at lead, not at dog*

#### COLLAPSING SUBMISSIVELY
While some dogs collapse because they are intimidated when brought back to the heel position, others regard it as a game, and roll over in play.

*Paw is raised submissively*

#### THE REMEDY
If the dog collapses, step backwards, and use a toy to excite the dog and induce it to get up.

*Toy is offered as reward*

# Refusing to Come

If your dog refuses to come to your call, find out the cause of its reluctance to obey before going back to recall training *(see page 58)*. Your dog may not have bonded to you; it may be bored, scavenging, or distracted by sexual opportunities; or it may have an excess of energy, or a desire to play with other dogs. Your dog may also be displaying dominant behaviour, or it may be afraid of either you or the lead. You should never call your dog to something that it considers unpleasant, such as a bath.

## On the scent
Dogs have a sophisticated sense of smell, and they acquire information about their environment through scenting. Allow the dog to sniff, call its name, tell it to sit, then command "Come".

*Dog sniffs ground for scent messages*

## Natural distraction
Even if the dog understands your recall command, it might choose to disregard it in favour of a sexual investigation. Neutered dogs are less interested in sex than entire ones, and are more likely to come when called.

*Sex-related scents are potent*

*Scent is sprayed below dog's nose*

## Scent obstruction
If the dog is an obsessive sniffer, spray perfume under its nose. This temporarily interferes with the sensitivity of the dog's scenting, so it will not be easily distracted.

## Utter boredom
If the dog does not consider you to be a worthy leader, it will not respond to your recall command. You should go back to the basic commands before continuing with recall training.

*Dog is bored and listless*

### Complete exhilaration

Young dogs tend to have a surplus of energy. If you have a young dog, make sure that it is well exercised before recalling it. If you are doubtful of the dog's compliance, keep it on an extending lead.

*Tongue hangs out with exhaustion following exercise*

### Extra Precautions

CAUTIOUS COMMAND

Only issue the "Come" command when you can enforce it. When the dog has had thorough recall training at home, graduate to outdoor areas. Initially, leave a long trailing or extending lead on the dog, to avoid grasping its collar *(see below)*, and always take food or toy rewards with you on outdoor trips.

FINAL REWARDS

Vary the play areas you take the dog to, since dogs can be obedient in one location, but not in others. Be energetic and enthusiastic when you call the dog, and praise it lavishly when it returns. At the end of the exercise period, rather than calling the dog to you, command it to sit, then go to it and put on its lead. Give the dog a reward before taking it home.

### Disobedience

Dogs can be temporarily distracted by an exciting activity. Attract the dog's attention by calling its name enthusiastically, then commanding it to come.

*Dog ignores owner's calls*

LEAD FEAR

You should never use the lead to discipline the dog, and never chastise it when it returns to you. Do not grab the dog by its collar, since it may think you are playing and try to avoid your grasp.

*Dog shrinks from lead*

### Successful scavenging

Scavenging and stealing can be more satisfying to the dog than your praise or food rewards. You should control this type of behaviour with either a long lead or a muzzle.

*Finding and chewing are rewarding activities*

### Rewarding obedience

Reinforce your recall command by holding the dog by its collar, and giving it a food treat. If necessary, use rewards such as food or a favourite toy to entice the dog back to you.

*Dog eagerly receives food reward*

### Playtime

Allow the dog the pleasure of playing with others, but observe its behaviour, and give the command "Come" if the play starts to become too boisterous.

# Chasing Vehicles

The desire to chase is part of normal canine behaviour, although the intensity of the desire varies from breed to breed, and among individuals. The instinct is stimulated by movement, and is reinforced if other dogs join in. It is possible to control chasing behaviour, but it can never be totally eliminated. You should not permit your dog to indulge in chasing, since it is a difficult problem to overcome, and can endanger its life.

## THE PROBLEM

*Tail is curled with excitement*

### Chasing cars

Chasing cars may be rewarding for the dog, but it is dangerous. The car drives away, so the dog is satisfied, but it is also on a potentially hazardous road.

*Bull Terriers are persistent chasers*

### Challenging cyclists

The sight of a cyclist stimulates many dogs to give chase. Because few cyclists ever stop, the dog considers the chase a success.

*Water is squirted while dog is still running*

## INSTANT SOLUTION

Ask a friend to cycle or drive past the dog. As the dog begins to chase, the cyclist should stop suddenly, squirt the dog with a water pistol, and say "No".

*JORDAN SIT*

*Long lead prevents dog from chasing*

*Cyclist goes slowly at first*

## REMEDIAL EXERCISE

1 Enlist the help of a friend to cycle or drive past for this exercise. As the cycle goes past slowly, command the dog to sit, holding a food reward in your hand. Make sure that the dog is under control during the exercise, using a lead or longline; it must not be given the opportunity to chase successfully.

2 Give the dog the food reward for sitting on command as the cyclist passes. Repeat the exercise until the dog reliably obeys your sit command, without attempting to chase, even as the speed of the cyclist increases. Then reward the dog with its favourite toy.

*Food is used as distraction and reward*

3 Repeat steps 1 and 2, using the toy as the distraction, with the cyclist travelling faster. Then progress to throwing the toy for the dog to retrieve *(see page 74)*, in the opposite direction to the cyclist, to distract the dog from chasing.

*Dog concentrates on toy*

---

## Breed Predispositions

### BUILT FOR SPEED

*The Greyhound is a classic sight hound*

Sight hounds, which are swift runners, and herding breeds, are natural chasers. Terriers are also instinctive chasers, but they often have short legs and cannot run fast.

### LASTING STAMINA

Arctic breeds of dog, such as Huskies and other spitzes, are slower than sight hounds, but have tremendous stamina, and are more likely to chase over long distances.

### SLOW BUT SURE

Scent hounds, like this Bloodhound, and gundogs, such as different breeds of pointer, setter, and retriever, are less likely to chase than other breeds.

# Chasing Animals

For thousands of years of evolution, dogs survived by chasing and killing other animals. Through selective breeding, humans have diminished this instinct, but it remains intense in some breeds and individuals. Chasing is natural canine behaviour, but it is also a serious problem, especially for livestock owners. One way of dealing with the problem involves training the dog to chase a safe object instead of other animals. If you are in any doubt about your ability to correct this problem, you should seek the advice of a professional dog trainer.

## CHASING LIVESTOCK

Unless the dog was socialized with other animals while it was still young (see page 19), you should anticipate problems when it meets potential prey. This dog stares intently at a goat, but it is on a lead and under the owner's control. Never allow a dog to walk off the lead on farmland unless you know from previous experience that it does not instinctively chase other animals. You should take similar precautions when it meets any other species for the first time.

*Dog intently and provocatively "eyeballs" goat*

*Dog is allowed to shake and pull on toy*

## THE REMEDY

1 The object of this exercise is to channel the dog's chase instinct into a controllable exercise. Experiment with different toys to discover which one the dog finds most exciting. Tease the dog vigorously with the toy.

2 In a quiet location, with the dog on a longline, throw the toy, but keep another exciting toy by your side. The dog will naturally chase the thrown toy.

*Longline gives owner control*

*Dog instinctively chases exciting object*

*Object has not been retrieved*

*"BILBO COME"*

*Second toy is waved invitingly*

### Dogs and Cats

#### GOOD FRIENDS

Dogs and cats enjoy each other's company if they are introduced to each other at an early age. Whenever possible, introduce a dog and a cat when the dog is under twelve weeks of age, and the cat is under seven weeks old.

If either animal is older, allow the resident to sniff the newcomer. First meetings should be supervised, and the dog should be prevented from chasing the cat.

#### COMPETITION

A resident animal may resent a new addition to your home, and regard it as competition for food or your affection. Reduce this risk by feeding both animals at the same time on the opposite sides of a closed door, or by feeding the dog on the ground and the cat at a higher level. Reward the dog with verbal and physical praise when it behaves with curiosity but gentleness with the cat. If the dog is not predatory or dominant towards the cat, the cat will eventually be in control.

**3** Before the dog reaches the toy, call its name and command it to return to you (see page 58). Be dramatic when recalling the dog, and wave the second toy to entice it to return. Then play with and praise the dog.

**4** Walk to the thrown toy and pick it up, holding the dog back with the lead. The dog will learn that the toys it chases belong to you. Repeat steps 2 to 4 in progressively more stimulating environments.

*Object is retrieved by owner*

*Dog watches owner pick up toy*

**5** Once the dog has been successfully trained not to chase an object of your choice, carry out a real retrieve exercise in the presence of livestock. Throw the toy in the opposite direction to the other animal, and encourage the dog to fetch it. You will soon be able to control the dog's instinct to chase by playing exciting retrieve games.

*Owner throws exciting toy*

*Longline is used at first*

*Dog eyes alternative "prey"*

*Toy has previously been used as a reward*

# Aggression Towards Dogs

Dominant aggression is most commonly directed towards another dog of the same sex. It is much more of a problem in males than in females, and occurs more frequently in some breeds than in others. This form of aggression is most likely to occur when the dog is on its own territory. Some dogs are simply social misfits, but more often the problem is sex-hormone-related, or has developed because of a lack of early and continuing socialization with other dogs. This can be difficult to deal with, and you may need professional help. Neutering at a young age reduces this behaviour in most male dogs.

## SIGNS OF AGGRESSION

### A fierce challenge

Dominantly aggressive dogs mean business. On most occasions, fighting is preceded by aggressive body posturing and growling. Unless one of the dogs backs down, a fight will ensue. During a fight, a dog is likely to bite whoever intervenes – even its owner.

*Barking madly is an intimidating preliminary to an attack*

### Eye contact

You should intervene the moment your dog makes eye contact with a potential adversary. A raised tail and intense concentration are indicators that a fight might begin.

### Between you and the dog

Some dogs will aggressively defend their owners. Standing between you and the other dog and pulling on the lead actually enhances the dog's feeling of aggression. The dog will eventually associate the feeling of straining on a lead with aggression, while it may show no aggression off the lead.

*Straining on the lead provokes more aggression*

### Tight-lead syndrome

Although you may instinctively try to keep the dog on a short lead when aggressive behaviour begins, this will often exacerbate the situation. Forcibly pulling the dog back will increase its aggression. You should turn your dog's head away so that it cannot make eye contact with the other dog.

## THE REMEDY

**1** Starting in a quiet environment, practise recall training with the dog *(see page 58)*. Retrain the dog on a longline or extending lead to return to you on command for a favourite toy.

*Ball-on-a-rope is a tempting toy*

*During retraining, dog's return is ensured by using longline*

**2** When the dog has been retrained to come to you in a quiet area, practise the exercise in an open space, with another dog in the distance. Reward the dog for not showing aggression to the other animal. Every day, reduce the distance between the dogs, rewarding your pet for its calm behaviour.

*Dog is kept on extending lead during training*

*Other dog is positioned some distance away at first*

## PREVENTION

### Deflect concentration
When you encounter a potentially aggressive situation, you should attract your dog's attention with its favourite toy, and then issue a sit command. Always reward the dog's good behaviour.

### Anticipate problems
Train the dog to wear a muzzle *(see pages 33 and 55)*. The muzzle physically prevents the dog from biting and diminishes its dominance.

*Dog concentrates on potential reward*

## Additional Information

*Testicles have been removed through a small incision in front of scrotum*

*Two normally descended testicles in an intact dog*

### MALE NEUTERING
Although spaying females is a sensible way to control unwanted pregnancies and behaviour, some people have unwarranted objections to castrating dogs – a far less invasive procedure. Surgically speaking, castration is a minor operation.

*Female bares her teeth aggressively*

### MATERNAL AGGRESSION
Female hormones heighten maternal aggression in some females. During twice-yearly periods of hormonal increase, some individuals become irritable, possessive of toys and bones, and protective of their dens. Neutering diminishes this form – but not all forms – of female aggression.

### SIMILAR PROBLEMS
Dogs that are equals are more likely to fight with each other than are dogs of different size, age, or sex. Some breeds, like Dobermanns, are more prone to aggression between equals than are other breeds.

# Aggression Towards People

Most dogs are content to be treated as subordinate members of the pack, and are willing to obey the commands of all members of their human family. Some dogs, however, are unwittingly taught by their owners that they are the real leaders of the pack. Leaders go through doors first, are fed first, and have their demands for comfort and affection met immediately. Once a dog thinks that it is the pack leader, it is likely to use aggression to enforce its control. You may require the services of a professional dog trainer in order to correct this behaviour.

## DOMINANT AGGRESSION

*Dominant dog stares directly at stranger*

This dog challenges an approaching person. Its aggression is based on dominance, although other dogs might act this way because they are frightened *(see page 100)*. The correction methods for these two problems are different, so make sure you use the right one.

## THE REMEDY

### No comforts
Making sure that the dominant dog wears a houseline at home, give the command "Off" if it climbs on to the furniture.

*Houseline prevents risk of bites*

### No risks
Using a muzzle or an adjustable head collar *(see page 33)* to ensure that the dog's mouth is closed will subdue the dog, reduce the risk of bites, and encourage it to respond to commands.

*Restrained dog quietly obeys "Sit" command*

*Dog's plea for attention is ignored*

### No response
Withdraw all affection from the dog. In order to regain your attention, the dog must do something for you. Disregard the dog until it stops making demands, then command it to sit and stroke it. The dog will quickly learn that you are in control.

*Dog allows itself to be groomed*

## Frequent grooming

Groom a dominant dog at least once a day, making sure that its mouth is closed *(see opposite)* and that it wears a houseline. You should also carry out at least two prolonged lying down sessions every day for three weeks *(see page 64).*

*(see opposite)* ... *(see page 64).*

### More Control

OPEN-PLAN BED

*Open-plan bedding is difficult to defend*

A dominantly aggressive dog should wear a houseline even when it is resting. Make sure that the dog's sleeping area is in the open, and not in a den-like corner or other enclosed space. Dogs feel more secure in dens, and a dominant dog's confidence should not be enhanced.

*Food is prepared but not given immediately*

*Dog sees that people eat first*

FETCH EXERCISES

Carry out pick up and retrieve exercises, since these help teach the dog that you are the leader. Ensure that the dog wears a houseline.

MEDICAL INTERVENTION

Dominant aggression is a potentially serious problem. Consult your vet, who may suggest that retraining will be most effective under medical supervision.

ANTIANXIETY PILLS

TRANQUILLIZER CAPSULES

ANTICONVULSANT TABLETS

HORMONE TABLETS

## Last to eat

In the wolf pack, the leader eats before his subordinates. Prepare the dog's food, but do not offer it until you have finished eating. Do not give the dog any food treats between meals during the weeks of retraining.

### Last to leave

Do not let the dog charge out of the door in front of you. Leaders go first, and you are the leader of the pack. The dog must adjust its pace to yours.

*Dog follows owner through doorway*

# Fear Biting

Although the snap of a fearful dog's jaws may look like dominant aggression *(see page 98)*, fear biting has different causes and requires different correction. The fear-biting dog is more apprehensive, and more likely to cower behind its owner's legs, than an aggressive animal. The problem results from inadequate socialization in some individuals, but it can be genetic in breeds like German Shepherd Dogs. Retraining of a fear-biting dog should be slow and cautious, and professional help is often useful.

*Dog's teeth are bared and its ears are flattened*

## FEARFUL AGGRESSION

The fear-biting dog often gives out mixed signals. The dog may cower near to its owner and wag its tail submissively, but then lunge forwards provocatively. Dogs with this behavioural problem usually have low self-esteem. Asserting your authority during training, as you would with a dominantly aggressive dog, only exaggerates the dog's lack of confidence.

## THE REMEDY

1 You will need the help of a friend or a professional trainer. The dog should be on a long lead, and should not have been fed before the exercise. Your friend should walk away, holding a food treat.

2 Allow the dog to walk towards your friend and take the food treat from the open palm. Your friend should not speak to the dog, and he should kneel with his back to it, avoiding any eye contact.

*Eyes look forwards*

3 Carry out steps 1 and 2 several times, then repeat them with your friend turning his body slightly towards the dog. There should still be no eye contact between him and the dog.

*Body is turned towards dog*

4 After successful attempts at the exercise over several days, proceed to the next stage. Repeat steps 1 and 2, with your friend turning to face the dog, again kneeling down.

*Intimidating eye contact is still avoided*

*Snack is offered to dog*

5 Now walk the dog towards your friend, who should be stationary. Avoiding eye contact with the dog, he should face it, offer the food treat, and step back. If the dog becomes fearful at this stage, go back to the previous stage and repeat it.

### Fear of Dogs

#### CANINE PHOBIA
Fear of other dogs may result from lack of early experience with other canines, or from being overprotected by owners; or it could be a consequence of having previously been frightened or bitten.

#### THE REMEDY
With the help of a friend who has a placid dog, go for a walk in an open space, and find the distance at which your dog does not show fear in the presence of the other dog. Reward the dog with food treats and affection when it displays relaxed behaviour. Every day, reduce the distance separating the two dogs until your dog walks fearlessly beside the other. Retraining of this kind usually takes three to six weeks.

6 Walk towards your friend, and as the dog takes the treat, praise it and stroke it along its body. Your friend should still be avoiding eye contact with the dog, but he can talk quietly to you. It will probably take several weeks to reach this stage.

*Dog confidently takes food while being touched*

*Dog is stroked along side*

7 Once the dog behaves confidently while you stroke it and your associate gives it a food treat, he should give the snack while stroking the dog's side. After repeating this exercise many times, make a subtle change. Still avoiding eye contact, your assistant should stroke the dog before giving the food reward.

# Guarding

Possessiveness is a behavioural problem that is most frequently encountered in dominant dogs. Pack leaders are more likely to decide that they own toys, food bowls, and resting places than are more submissive dogs, but there are also breed predispositions.

For example, terriers are possessive of food, toys, and rest areas. Avoid confrontations with a possessive dog by not giving it toys, and not allowing it to sit on your furniture. You should treat problems by withdrawing affection, reteaching basic commands, and keeping your dog on a training lead.

## GUARDING FOOD

This dog growls possessively and dominantly as its owner approaches its food bowl. The dog feels that it is pack leader, and leaders protect their possessions – they do not share. Both males and females are susceptible to indulging in guarding behaviour. If you back down when the dog growls, it will learn that this behaviour is effective, and will be encouraged to use it more frequently.

*Dog threatens with a growl*

## THE REMEDY

1 When carrying out this exercise, make sure that the dog is held on a training lead by a friend or a member of the family. Do not feed the dog before the exercise. Offer the dog a bowl containing a small amount of bland food, such as rice, instead of a full bowl of tasty food. Let the dog sniff the food.

*Food bowl only contains rice*

2 With the dog watching, introduce a small amount of tastier food. Repeat this exercise every time you feed the dog, and after several days it will welcome your visit to its food bowl.

*Dog watches as owner adds food*

*Tasty food is put into bowl*

## GUARDING FURNITURE

Dominant dogs choose their resting places. This dog has chosen a chair, and is guarding it, along with a toy that it considers its own. You should never pull on a dominant dog's collar, since it may try to bite.

### Guarding the Family

Stranger approaches owner

Dog growls protectively

#### OWNER-POSSESSIVE
Although humans appreciate the security that dogs provide, some dogs become extremely possessive of their owners – especially if they are of the opposite sex.

#### THE REMEDY
If the dog becomes too possessive, keep it on a lead so that you are able to control it when visitors arrive. Leave a food snack near the front door for a friend to bring in. As the visitor enters, command the dog to sit and stay. Instruct the visitor to avoid eye contact with the dog, and to crouch down and offer the food reward.

Dog stops growling in order to take treat

## "OFF"

### THE REMEDY

Keep the dog's training lead on throughout the day; this will ensure that you have complete control. Induce the dog to leave the chair by commanding "Off", and offering a food reward. A slight jerk on the lead may be necessary at first.

Food is used as inducement for dog to jump down

## GUARDING TOYS

Some dogs will guard toys, and will refuse to relinquish them. You should avoid tug-of-war games with these dogs, since they always play to win.

### THE REMEDY

1 With a tasty treat in one hand and a toy in the other, encourage the dog to take the toy.

2 Issue the command "Give", and when the dog releases the toy, reward it by saying "Good dog" and giving the food. Repeat the exercise immediately by giving the toy back to the dog, then commanding "Give" again.

Dog is rewarded with snack

# Rivalry Between Dogs

Humans are not the only species to experience emotions – dogs have them, too. Jealousy and rivalry are most likely to occur in dogs of the same sex, size, age, and temperament. They may squabble over bones, sleeping areas, or for their owner's attention. Dogs cannot share covetable items, so each dog should have its own bed and food bowl – although a water bowl can be shared. Some dominant breeds, such as Dobermanns, experience more sibling rivalry than other breeds. Neutering the underdog may be necessary to increase the difference between two resident male dogs.

## SIBLING RIVALRY

**Arguing over possessions**
Bones are the objects most likely to provoke arguments between littermates. Avoid potential problems either by not giving bones at all, or by giving them in separate rooms. It does not matter how many bones you offer; one dog will always want the other's bone.

*Dog growls aggressively because it wants the other dog's bone*

*Dogs eat without making eye contact*

**Avoid eye contact**
Reduce rivalry by feeding your dogs together, but ensure that they face in opposite directions. Each dog will learn that it will receive a food reward if it eats with the other without fighting. Always put the dominant dog's bowl down first.

**Mutual rewards**
If the dogs have similar personalities, and there are no clear indications that one is dominant, issue joint commands such as "Sit", and reward both dogs at the same time. They will learn to be obedient in each other's presence.

*Dominant dog is greeted and rewarded*

*Less dominant dog waits to be greeted by owner*

*Mutual rewards are given without provoking jealousy*

**Greet the dominant dog first**
There is no democracy in the canine world. If the dogs give you indications about which one is top dog, you should acknowledge their relationship by greeting the leader first. This reduces the dominant dog's need to show its authority.

## JEALOUSY

### Introducing a puppy

Although most dogs eventually enjoy the introduction of another dog into the home, there may be some jealousy at first. Reduce problems by adhering to your routines as much as possible. Give the resident dog plenty of attention in the presence of the new arrival; it will soon associate the puppy with pleasurable activities.

*Resident dog receives attention*

*Puppy is disregarded*

### Mutual enjoyment

Feed the resident dog and the new puppy together, but make sure that there is no eye contact between them. Feed the older dog as often as the puppy, but without increasing the total quantity of its food.

*Dog gets no response from owner*

### Gentle disregard

When the new puppy is absent, ignore the older dog. It will learn to associate the presence of the puppy with increased attention from you.

### Allow escape

Puppies can be exhilarating, but also exasperating. The resident dog may become tired of the constant pestering from the youngster. Set up a barrier so that the older dog can escape from the puppy's demands.

*Puppy is restricted by barrier*

### Personal Space

All dogs need their own private territories, somewhere they can go when they are tired, or when they want to be alone. Provide each dog with the security of its own bed. You should not allow one dog to use the other's bed, since this can lead to disputes. Each bed should contain comfortable, clean, washable bedding.

*Dog is content in its own bed*

# Problems with Sex

Excessive canine sexual behaviour is perfectly natural, but it can sometimes be annoying. The sex-related problems of urine marking, vagrancy, territory guarding, fighting with other dogs, and overprotectiveness occur most frequently in male dogs, and are easiest to control in neutered animals. Breeding a dog so that it can experience sex is counter productive, since it may result in excessive sexual behaviour later in the dog's life. Neutering females generally has little effect on behaviour, although it can increase dominant behaviour in naturally dominant bitches. However, simple sexual activity in both sexes can be controlled through careful training.

## SEXUAL SUBSTITUTE

*Dog grasps owner's leg*

Female dogs do not allow males to mount them unless they are in season. Few dogs ever meet bitches in heat, so they often attempt to mount their owners. Bitches also indulge in this activity. It is harmless – but annoying – behaviour, which often begins before a puppy has reached puberty. If you allow a puppy to mount limbs, the behaviour will be difficult to correct in adulthood.

## THE REMEDY

*Oversexed dog should wear lead or houseline at home during retraining*

1 Every time the dog tries to mount a person's arm or leg, say "No", remove it using the lead, and isolate it for one minute. When the dog is oversexed, it finds any physical contact – even a reprimand – potentially gratifying, so avoid touching it.

2 Isolation is a symbolic gesture, and should only be carried out for very short periods of time. After one minute, allow the dog back into your company, but ignore it.

*Dog receives no attention from owner*

3 After disregarding the dog for a few minutes, command it to sit, give it a reward, and play with it. The fact that the dog has mounted your leg indicates that it is in need of physical and mental stimulation. You should make sure that the dog receives enough exercise.

*Tug toy is a suitable diversion*

## MOUNTING OBJECTS

*Dog clasps rug and thrusts with pelvis*

If a dog is frustrated in its attempt to mount dogs and people, it may turn to furry toys, cushions, or rugs. This behaviour is perfectly normal, but it can be damaging to articles, and offensive to some people.

### THE REMEDY

As the dog thrusts on the rug, command "Off", and squirt it with a water pistol. Most dogs find the water spray disconcerting. You should acknowledge that the dog is bored and frustrated, and provide it with mental and physical activity.

*Unexpected water spray diverts dog's attention*

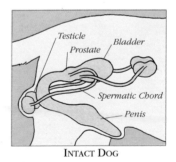

## MOUNTING VISITORS

Some dogs will mount a visitor's limbs simply to get attention. Others will do so because they have learned that they are not allowed to indulge in the activity with members of the family.

*Dog pants with excitement*

### Neutering

If the dog is not to be used for breeding, and if it has any bad habits related to sex hormone, discuss with your vet the advantages of having the dog neutered. Neutering does not alter a dog's basic personality; it simply lessens the likelihood of sex-related problems.

*Testicle* *Bladder* *Prostate* *Spermatic Chord* *Penis*

**INTACT DOG**

### THE REMEDY

Pull the dog away by its lead, and shut it in another room until your visitor has left. Alternatively, repeat the exercises of isolation, disregard, and command *(see opposite)*. Avoid embarrassment by keeping the dog in another room whenever you have visitors, or by putting on its lead, and instructing your visitor not to pet or excite it.

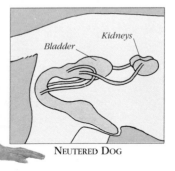

*Bladder* *Kidneys*

**NEUTERED DOG**

# Problems in Cars

Some dogs enjoy car travel, both because they find the journeys exciting, and because car trips often end in exercise and meetings with other dogs. Some dogs hate travelling in cars because of the uncontrolled motion, resulting in nausea. Try to take your dog on frequent, short trips so that it becomes accustomed to the car. If your dog dribbles or experiences car sickness, do not feed it before a trip, and protect the car with newspapers or old towels. Reprimand your dog if it shows signs of defending the car as its own territory.

**Beginning the journey**
Entice the dog into the car with food (if it does not suffer from nausea) or a toy, but do not overexcite the dog before you embark on a trip.

*Dog waits before jumping into car*

*Dog pants contentedly*

*No nausea-induced dribbling*

**A second home**
At first, provide the dog with a toy and a bowl of food in the car, so that it associates car travel with enjoyable activities. Remove the food bowl before the journey.

*Newspaper protects car seat*

## Excessive barking

If the dog is unruly in the car and barks excessively, someone should sit with it and command it to be quiet when necessary *(see page 66)*.

*As dog howls, owner firmly commands "Quiet"*

## Destructive digging

Left on its own in the car, the dog may dig into and chew the interior. Spray the upholstery and seatbelts with a non-toxic, bitter substance *(see page 31)*, and provide the dog with a toy to chew.

*Dog's nails can destroy seat fabric*

## Sunblind

A sunblind on the car window keeps the sun off the dog. It is also useful for calming down excitable dogs, since it obscures their view and makes the ride less stimulating.

*Sunblind is easily attached to car window*

## Further Precautions

*Crates fit best in hatch backs*

*Dog is content and relaxed*

### TRANSPORT CRATE

Crate-trained dogs can undertake car journeys in a transport crate. In addition to offering safety, a crate will eliminate any destructive activity. The dog will feel secure and relaxed, but you should also provide it with a stimulating toy.

### SIMPLE CONTROL

Try muzzling the dog to prevent excessive barking and destructive behaviour. Tying its lead to the seatbelt anchor will also help, since it will prevent the dog from moving around too much. Alternatively, specially designed seatbelts will limit the dog's movement, prevent it from distracting the driver, and can reduce the risk of it being injured in an accident.

### CARS CAN KILL

Never leave the dog unattended in a car in warm weather; even parking in the shade and leaving a window partly open is not safe. Dogs have poor control of their body temperatures and can suffer potentially fatal heatstroke as a result of overheating. Even during cold weather, you should not leave the dog alone in a car with the heater on.

### PROVIDE REFRESHMENT

Make sure that you have a container of water in the car, especially during long journeys. You should stop every few hours to allow the dog to drink and relieve itself.

# Nervousness

Nervous behaviour is most common in small breeds and in dogs that were isolated when they were young. However, it also occurs unexpectedly in many other dogs, for a variety of reasons. Fear of noises such as backfiring cars, thunder, or fireworks can develop – even in placid hunting breeds like retrievers. Some dogs become frightened when they see moving objects they do not recognize, such as skateboards or prams. Other dogs are afraid of people on crutches or in wheelchairs, and although physical abuse may be the reason why a dog is nervous of hands, in most such cases there is no history of abuse.

## FEAR OF NOISES

On hearing loud noises like thunder, many dogs become apprehensive and try to hide. An owner's natural reaction is to comfort the nervous dog and distract it from the source of the fear. However, this can exaggerate the dog's fearful response, since it learns that when it behaves nervously it is rewarded with contact from its owner, soothing words, and even food.

*Dog has fearful expression*

*Tail hangs limp and tucks under*

## THE REMEDY

*Food reward is given for good behaviour*

Make a sound recording of the noise that frightens the dog. Under controlled circumstances, when you know the noise is not going to occur naturally, start to play the recording. Play it quietly at first, and reward the dog for not displaying nervous behaviour. Over several weeks, gradually increase the intensity of the sound until it is as loud as the noise that the dog is frightened of.

*Dog is on lead for complete control*

## FEAR OF OBJECTS

Dogs are sometimes nervous of unfamiliar objects, especially those that move. Dogs that live in families with no children are often afraid of prams, and they may cower or try to run away when they see one.

## THE REMEDY

1 Place a tasty morsel on the floor near to the pram. Do not feed the dog before the exercise, so that it will want to eat the snack. Place treats closer to the pram, and after several sessions the dog should put its head under the pram to eat them.

*Titbit is placed under pram*

*Dog eats from bowl*

2 Once the dog willingly takes titbits from under the pram, graduate to placing its food bowl there. During corrective training, move the pram occasionally and reward the dog for showing no fear.

## FEAR OF HANDS

Nervous dogs often experience conflicts; they want to greet people but are afraid of hands, so they shy away.

*There is a look of trepidation in dog's eyes*

*Eye contact is avoided*

## THE REMEDY

1 Place your palm containing a food treat on the ground in front of the dog. If you think the dog could bite, follow the remedy suggested for fear-biting dogs *(see page 100).*

2 Once the dog consistently and willingly takes the food from the ground, reduce the distance between you and the dog, and move to its side.

### Submissive Behaviour

#### SUBMISSIVE URINATION
Very nervous dogs roll over submissively, and even urinate, when presented with frightening demands or situations. If the dog behaves this way during training, you are being too forceful. Do not pet or touch the dog, since this could intimidate it further.

*Urination is a sign of abject submission*

#### THE REMEDY
You should get down to the dog's level, in order to restore its confidence. Then entice the dog to get up, using a favourite toy. Playing retrieve enables the dog to leave its submissive position without being physically handled by you, which can make it feel even more submissive. If the dog rolls over and urinates when you greet it, ignore it until it calms down.

*Rolling over is submissive play activity*

# Boredom

Dogs are gregarious social animals, and their senses, minds, and bodies need stimulation. If you return home to scenes of canine destruction, do not assume that your pet has displayed this behaviour as revenge for being left alone. Dogs are incapable of carrying out premeditated crimes against property. Howling, digging, destroying, jumping, and rhythmically pacing back and forth are all signs of anxiety. You can prevent problems associated with boredom by providing natural outlets for your dog's physical and mental needs.

## SEPARATION ANXIETY

*Mouth is raised to produce a howl*

### Digging to escape
While some dogs dig to bury bones, and others to create cool pits to lie in, many dig simply out of frustration.

*Digging requires concentration and dexterity*

### Howling for attention
Wolf cubs howl to attract the attention of their mothers. In the same way, the bored, frustrated, and understimulated dog barks or howls to gain its owner's attention when it is left alone.

*Shaking rug vigorously is emotionally rewarding*

### Rhythmic jumping
In a garden, a bored dog may amuse itself by jumping to look over the fence. Separation anxiety causes some dogs to pace back and forth, urine mark, howl, and dig.

*Ears point forwards eagerly*

### Anxious destruction
Dogs can be dramatically destructive, scratching off wallpaper, chewing car interiors, and destroying rugs, clothing, and household linen. This behaviour is most common in underexercised and insecure dogs, especially rescued individuals that are emotionally dependent on their owners.

# PREVENTING PROBLEMS

*Dog sniffs for any new smells*

### Using the senses
Before leaving the dog alone, give it plenty of mental and physical exercise. Exhausted dogs are less likely to bark, dig, and destroy than those with excess energy.

### Meeting other dogs
You should not isolate a dog from other canines. Arrange controlled meetings to ensure that the dog is well socialized with others.

*Dog is apprehensive at first*

### Playing games
When you leave the dog alone, give it a toy that it is obsessed with. Rubbing the toy in your hands to cover it with your scent makes the dog feel more secure.

*Chewing a toy is a rewarding activity*

### Off to work
Dogs should not be left at home alone all day, since they enjoy activity. Taking the dog to your workplace, if possible, will reduce boredom and minimize destructive behaviour.

*Dog has its own personal space*

*All dogs are walked on leads*

### A helping hand
If you must leave the dog alone for long periods, prevent boredom-related problems from developing by employing a professional dog walker. Alternatively, enlist the services of a friend who can exercise the dog frequently.

## Further Prevention

PLANNING AHEAD

Check the dog's behaviour by leaving it alone in a room, together with a toy. After a few minutes, go back into the room and praise the dog for not showing signs of boredom, such as barking, pacing, or digging at the door. Repeat this exercise in different rooms and over varying periods of time, until the dog can be left alone without exhibiting any signs of anxiety.

QUIET FAREWELL

Always leave quietly. Drawing the curtains and leaving a radio or television on will mask distracting outdoor noises. It is important to remember that even well-behaved dogs can have separation problems in new homes.

# Cures for Boredom

You will find it extremely difficult to eliminate boredom-related problems unless you simultaneously eliminate the causes. Give your dog the opportunity to exercise, explore, sniff, scent, and urine mark. Increase the self-confidence of dogs that fear being left alone. Consider neutering if your male dog's barking, digging, escaping, or destroying is sex related. Only when the cause is removed will you be in a position to retrain your pet to overcome its antisocial behaviour. It is important to remember that your dog's behaviour is a result of anxiety and frustration, and not a means of revenge.

## HOWLING

"QUIET"

### Command training

If the dog persistently barks and howls when left alone, train it to respond to the "Quiet" command (*see page 66*), then set up mock departures. Attract the dog's attention, command it to be quiet, and stand outside the front door. If the dog barks, drop a tin tray or throw a bunch of keys at the door in order to startle it. Return and praise the dog when it is quiet, then leave again. This exercise takes time and patience.

*Owner gives visual command*

*Eye contact is maintained*

*Dog has been commanded to sit*

## DIGGING

*Digging is instinctive behaviour*

### Rest follows feeding

Dogs are less likely to be active on full stomachs than on empty ones, so they will indulge less in digging behaviour if they have been fed. If the dog is left alone during the day, feed it in the morning rather than in the evening.

*Large meal can reduce desire for physical activity*

### Creative activity

Constructively redirect the dog's natural instinct to dig in flower beds or on the lawn by providing it with its own sand pit.

## JUMPING

### Roadblock
Prevent the dog from jumping up at the garden fence by placing chicken wire on bricks along the base. Make sure that the gauge of the wire is too small for the dog's feet to slip through. The wire will make digging and jumping difficult for the dog.

*Wire provides insecure footing*

*Use empty tin cans on a rope*

*Dog sees obstacle and is reluctant to jump*

### Separation Anxiety
Dogs that lack confidence – particularly individuals that have been through animal shelters – are most likely to bark, dig, and destroy when left alone. These insecure animals need gentle handling, and their anxiety-related activities take time to cure. Gradually, over a period of many weeks, increase the periods of separation, always leaving the dog with a toy that you have rubbed in your hands. Discipline the dog only if you see it misbehaving – never after. Poor timing on your part will confuse the dog further.

*Rescued dog cowers apprehensively when left alone*

### Noisy intervention
String several tin cans on a rope, about 1 metre (3 ft) above the ground and about 30 centimetres (12 in) from the fence. If the dog jumps and hits the string, the noise of the rattling tin cans will give instant, startling discipline.

## CHEWING

### Controlled environment
When leaving home, put the dog in its own crate with a favourite toy *(see page 34)*. You could also apply taste deterrent *(see page 31)* to the areas that the dog regularly chews.

### Physical activity
Dogs need physical activity, and the best way to reduce the problems associated with boredom is to give them daily exercise.

*Dog is content to chew toys while confined to crate*

# Jumping Up

A puppy greets its mother by jumping up to lick her face. Dogs, especially adolescents between six and eighteen months old, sometimes try to do the same to humans. Excitement usually triggers this activity. Labrador Retrievers and poodles tend to jump up for affection, while breeds like Rottweilers do so to show their dominance. Do not encourage your dog's natural inclination to jump up by slapping your thighs and raising your voice when you return home. Tell children to keep their hands by their sides. If you behave calmly, your dog is also more likely to do so.

## JUMPING EXCITEDLY

*Dog looks directly into owner's eyes*

Jumping occurs most frequently when dogs are excited. Homecoming, picking up the dog's lead, or the arrival of a visitor can all stimulate jumping up. Although often an activity of young dogs, this is also the behaviour of understimulated individuals. Reduce the likelihood of your dog behaving this way by ensuring that it receives frequent exercise.

## THE REMEDY

*Dogs of this size can knock people over*

*Owner avoids stimulating eye contact*

*Owner uses visual as well as verbal command*

1 You should begin to correct jumping behaviour by reinforcing the dog's obedience to the "Sit" and "Stay" commands (see page 56). Rather than using a negative command such as "Off", enter the room and command the dog to sit. Do not raise your voice or wave your arms, since both activities stimulate the dog.

2 Reward the dog when it sits on command, but avoid stroking the top of its head, since it may try to lick your face. Instead, crouch down to the dog's level and stroke it briskly along its flanks or under its chin. Praise the dog for its quiet behaviour. Practise this exercise until the dog no longer jumps up.

## CANINE MISSILE

*Dog leaps with excitement*

While some dogs simply jump up to lick their owners' faces, others launch themselves through the air towards people. This is normal play activity between dogs, but it is potentially dangerous to people.

## THE REMEDY

You should ignore the flamboyant greeting and, avoiding eye contact, walk past the dog. When the dog's feet are back on the ground, command it to sit, then get down to its level. Praise the dog's obedience.

## JUMPING UP ON VISITORS

1 If the dog persistently jumps up on visitors when they arrive, put on its lead before opening the front door. Give the command "Sit".

2 Ask a friend to bring food rewards for the dog on the next visit. The dog should receive a reward from the visitor upon sitting obediently after his arrival.

### Additional Information

#### MEETING CHILDREN

*Dog obeys owner's commands*

*Child quietly greets dog*

Some dogs are more inclined to jump up on children than on adults, because children's faces are closer, and they appear to act in a more exciting manner. Introduce the dog to a child under controlled conditions, with the dog on a lead. Instruct the child not to raise her arms to her face, but to keep them by her sides. Reward the dog for not jumping up.

#### BEGGING ATTENTION

Some dogs – especially small breeds – jump up, bark, whine, or lick, in order to attract attention or to beg for food. This is canine bad manners, and you should not allow a dog to do this. Never feed the dog from the table, and do not respond to its demands. If you respond, the dog will learn that the behaviour is fruitful. Reduce the dog's dependence on you by making sure that other members of the family, as well as friends, play with it and feed it.

#### FORCEFUL CONTROL

Always use positive methods to control the dog's behaviour. You should never knee the dog in its chest, step on its hind feet, or squeeze its forepaws when it jumps up. You can control the dog's behaviour with common sense. Be firm, but not angry.

# Excited Behaviour

Dogs sometimes adopt frenzied behavioural patterns through excitement. They bark hysterically, chase their tails, chew stones, compulsively groom themselves, or demand to be picked up. Consult your vet to ensure that the hysterical behaviour is not caused by a medical condition. With that assurance, you should proceed with basic retraining.

## EXCESSIVE BARKING

Many dogs act like canine alarms – barking when they hear unexpected noises. Some dogs, however, especially terriers, poodles and Lhasa Apsos, become chronically excessive barkers unless they are taught to control their behaviour. The barking often becomes rhythmic, and may only stop momentarily on a command from the owner. To the hysterical dog, your shout of "Quiet" appears to be an attempt to join in.

*Owner gives food reward when dog is quiet*

## THE REMEDY

**Voice control**
Go back to teaching the "Speak" and "Quiet" commands *(see page 66)*, in controlled situations. Enlist the services of a friend, who can ring your doorbell while you practise the exercise.

**Mild punishment**
Dramatic gestures are sometimes necessary. As the dog barks, squirt a non-toxic, non-irritating, but unpleasant-tasting, substance into its mouth, taking care to avoid its eyes.

## TAIL CHASING

When highly excited, some dogs, especially Bull Terriers, chase their tails. Although there is a strong genetic component to the behaviour, the activity is self-rewarding and increases in frequency unless it is stopped.

*Dog twirls around until it catches its tail*

## THE REMEDY

*Dog concentrates on owner's new reward*

Divert the tail chaser's attention by offering another reward. Command the dog to sit, and when it obeys reward it with a chew toy or food snack. You should seek veterinary advice if the problem persists.

# DEMANDING ATTENTION

## Pick-me-up

Insecure dogs sometimes become hysterical if they are not picked up. This is most likely to occur in dependent dogs, especially when they find themselves in new environments. The dogs' demands become increasingly obsessive if they are not picked up, and the behaviour becomes chronic, since the adrenalin released acts as its own reward.

*Dog persistently scratches to attract owner's attention*

*Dog jumps surprisingly high*

## Jack-in-the-box

Some dogs repetitively bounce high in the air in an attempt to lick a human face. You should not be domineering with these dogs, since they need to gain more self-esteem.

## THE REMEDY

1 If the dog persistently and obsessively jumps up, or scratches you with its paws, quietly leave the room. The dog will be surprised by your sudden departure.

*Dog is startled into being quiet*

*Dog now listens to and obeys owner*

2 A minute later, and while the dog is still calm, return, and reassert control over the dog by commanding it to sit. You should always reward the dog's good behaviour.

## Compulsive Behaviour

### BARKING

Not all barking is compulsive; most barking is, in fact, normal and natural. Dogs bark greetings to us and to other dogs. They also have alarm barks, threat barks, and communal barks. Only uncontrolled or excessive barking is wrong. If the dog is barking excessively and will not stop, hold it by the scruff of the neck, obtain direct eye contact, give it a quick, firm shake, and say "Quiet".

### LICKING

Obsessive licking of the forepaws can be a grooming disorder, similar to human grooming disorders, such as obsessive hand washing. Consult your vet, who might want to use specific drugs to control this activity. The problem is particularly common in Labrador Retrievers and Dobermanns.

*Dog compulsively licks its leg*

# Food Problems

From the time your dog enters your home, train it to eat only from its own bowl. Feeding the dog after people have eaten helps to teach it to obey commands, since it learns that humans are more dominant than dogs. Do not leave food in accessible places, or feed the dog from the dining table, and make sure that your rubbish bin has a secure lid. If eating problems do develop, they are not usually difficult to overcome.

## STEALING FOOD

It is instinctive for dogs to look for food, and rewarding for them to find something tasty and to eat it. What humans consider to be rubbish is often delightful to a dog.

## THE REMEDY

1 If the dog scavenges in the rubbish bin, set up situations that will entice it to carry out a raid in your presence. As the dog does this, firmly give the command "Leave", so that it understands that the activity is not permitted.

*Obedient dog willingly obeys command*

2 Put the lid firmly on the bin. Then make the rubbish less enticing by spraying the bin with a non-toxic, bitter-tasting substance *(see page 31)*. Let the dog investigate the sprayed bin. For this method to be effective, the unpleasant taste of the bin must be greater than the reward of a raid.

*This is a harmless but bitter-tasting spray*

*No attractive rubbish is visible*

# BEGGING

*Paw is used to attract owner's attention*

Dogs that come to the table and beg for food can be a real nuisance. Giving an occasional treat from the table is actually worse than responding to the dog every time you sit down to a meal. Constant habits are easier to alter than those that occur occasionally.

## THE REMEDY

**1** Train the dog to take food only when permitted. Command it to sit while you prepare its food – away from the table.

*Dog waits until command to take food is given*

**2** Put the food on the floor, but keep the dog in the sit position until you release it with the command "Take it" or "OK".

---

## "Disgusting" Habits

### EATING ANIMAL DROPPINGS

This is a disgusting habit to us, but animal droppings can be genuinely nourishing to dogs. Scavenging herbivore droppings from horses, rabbits, and deer, is natural behaviour for some dogs – especially Labrador Retrievers and Golden Retrievers. Use standard obedience training to overcome this habit. If you see the dog looking with interest at an animal dropping, give the command "No". If the dog picks it up, give the command "Drop".

### EATING DOG DROPPINGS

Eating its own or other dog droppings is a more dangerous habit than the one above. The dog can pick up intestinal parasites; it can also create a bacterial overgrowth condition in its intestines, resulting in chronic diarrhoea. Always clean up after the dog, but to assist in overcoming the problem, leave a recently passed stool and taint it with Tabasco sauce.

*Dog will find peppery sauce unpleasant*

---

# REFUSING FOOD

*Dog refuses to eat new variety of food*

Some dogs will refuse to eat the food they are offered. This is common among toy breeds, but also occurs in large, lean breeds, such as the Saluki. Dogs can go without food for longer periods than humans.

## THE REMEDY

FULL BOWL    SMALLER QUANTITY    EVEN SMALLER QUANTITY    SMALLER QUANTITY AGAIN    FRESH WATER

A healthy dog will not starve if food is present. With your vet's permission, offer food for ten minutes then remove any uneaten food. Repeat the exercise daily with smaller amounts, until the food is eaten.

# Effective Training

If you want to be an effective trainer, your dog must think of you as leader of the pack. If a dog decides what and when it wants to be fed, where it wants to sleep, or when it wants to be picked up, and you respond, then even the most naturally submissive dog will soon believe that it is the dominant member of the household.

Your dog will only pay attention to you if it respects you. If you keep a record of how you behave with your dog, it will help you discover whether or not you have laid the groundwork for effective dog training. Help in training your dog is always available. Contact your local veterinary clinic for details of classes in your area.

## PROFESSIONAL HELP

### Puppy socialization classes
Open to owners and puppies under 16 weeks old, these weekly classes are an ideal method of introducing young dogs to other puppies and to people. Puppy parties provide a firm foundation for more formal training.

### Basic obedience classes
These classes are open to older dogs, but also to puppies that

have not attended socialization classes. They are usually held by experienced dog trainers, and teach both you and your dog the basics of canine obedience.

### Advanced training classes
Although basic training is perfectly adequate for most dogs, advanced training gives you more refined control of your pet. By introducing both you and your dog to the enjoyment of canine agility, tracking, purpose-made activity games, and other dog sports, advanced training helps to develop the full potential of the partnership between you and your canine companion.

### Kennel training
Some kennels offer residential training courses for dogs, where your dog is trained in your absence. Although residential training can be useful for specific and specialized work, it is always best if you and your dog are able to train together.

### Personal training
Some behavioural problems, for example certain forms of aggression or livestock chasing, are so serious that they warrant the help of a personal trainer. Your vet should be able to suggest someone.

### Veterinary help
If you do not plan to breed from your dog, consider neutering. Early neutering reduces, or even eliminates, the risk of mammary tumours and womb infection in females, and prostate problems and perianal tumours in males. Neutered dogs also tend to be most responsive to training. If your dog is not behaving normally, or if behavioural problems develop, you should consult your vet. Changed behaviour might be a sign of illness, and in exceptional circumstances your vet may suggest a short course of medication for certain behavioural disorders.

# TRAINING RECORD

| | | | | |
|---|---|---|---|---|
| Where did you acquire your dog? | | Breeder/Friend | | Advertisement/Shelter/Pet shop |
| How old was your dog when you acquired it? | | Under 26 weeks | | Over 26 weeks |
| Has your female dog been neutered? | | No | | Yes |
| Has your male dog been neutered? | | Yes | | No |
| Have you previously owned a dog? | | Yes | | No |
| When is your dog fed? | | Set times | | On demand |
| Does your dog eat after you? | | Yes | | No |
| When does your dog relieve itself? | | Set times | | On demand |
| Where does your dog sleep? | | Kitchen/Outdoors | | Bedroom/On bed |
| How often is your dog groomed? | | Frequently | | Infrequently |
| How does your dog react to grooming? | | Dog is willing | | Dog is unwilling |
| When is your dog exercised? | | Set times | | On demand |
| How long is the exercise period? | | More than 1 hour/day | | Less than 1 hour/day |
| Do you have off-lead control? | | Yes | | No |
| Where are the dog's toys kept? | | In toy container | | On floor |
| How often does your dog play with other dogs? | | Frequently | | Infrequently |
| How often does your dog play with other people? | | Frequently | | Infrequently |
| How often is your dog left at home alone? | | Infrequently | | Frequently |
| How often does your dog have special playtime with you? | | Frequently | | Infrequently |

If your answers to these questions are mainly in the first column, you are well on your way to effective dog training. If most of your answers are in the second column, you will benefit from professional advice from an experienced dog handler.

# Index

# Acknowledgments

**Author's Acknowledgments**
Anyone who says that writing is a lonely business has never had the opportunity to write a book like this. After months of preparation, the team of people involved in the book finally get to the photographic studio. At this stage, Tracey Williams, the Project Editor, also acts as stage manager; she makes sure that the right dogs and people arrive and are in place at the right time. Tim Scott, the Art Editor, is also the set designer; he monitors not only the props, but also the appearance of the models – both canine and human. The cameraman is Tim Ridley, and the director is my agent, Patricia Holden White.

As well as being one of London's most experienced and respected literary agents, by sheer good fortune Patricia Holden White is also one of Great Britain's leading dog trainers. We have both been influenced by the logic of sensible, pragmatic, and realistic dog trainers like John Rogerson and John Fisher in Great Britain, and the Monks of New Skete and Terry Ryan in the United States. Showing dedication above and beyond the call of literary duty, Pat attended virtually every photo shoot, making sure that owners and dogs performed properly.

Thanks to all of these people, and to Krystyna Mayer, the Managing Editor, and Derek Coombes, the Managing Art Editor, who were always available to sort out any unexpected problems. My gratitude also to the dog models and their owners, often clients and patients of mine, who willingly agreed to participate in the production of this book.

**Patricia Holden White** would like to thank everyone who has contributed their time, help, and loan of dogs to this book. In particular, thank you to members of the Hammersmith Dog Obedience Club; John Uncle and the members of his London Canine Dog Training Establishment; and Alan Menzies and the members of the Alan Menzies Dog Training Club. Thanks also to Lois Hunter of ACA Books and Supplies (Stambourne) for supplying some of the training equipment.

The kind and non-confrontational methods used in this book are based on an amalgamation of training philosophies. I am grateful to Roy Hunter, John Rogerson, Gail Fisher, and Terry Ryan for their extraordinary insight into dog behaviour, and their unselfish sharing of information in furthering better dog training. And, of course, to Bruce Fogle for the fun of working together on this book.

**Dorling Kindersley's Acknowledgments**
Dorling Kindersley would like to thank the following people for lending dogs and for modelling:

Malcolm and Melissa Ambrose (*Jemima*); Hermione Austin (*Tigger* and *Erasmus*); Gill Bartlett (*Katie*); Jessica Berkeley; Vicky Bickell; Charlotte Bishop (*Floss*); Ian and Rebecca Bowman (*Dottie*); Mrs. Cardiel (*Dylan*); Pamela Clarke (*Freo*); Suzanne Collins (*Karma* and *Harvey*); Keeley Daines (*Jordan*); Christine Davis (*Spike* and *Thomas*); Mel Dawson (*Digby*); Mrs. Fielding (*Benjy*); Bruce Fogle and Julia Foster (*Liberty* and *Lexington*); Sonia Funcheon (*Tessa*); Donald Goddard (*Violet*); Nicholas Goodall; Barbara Greeves; Michael Guest (*Ben*); Thomas, William, and Daniel Hunter; Billie Ingram (*Arthur*); Rosalind Ingram (*Diva*); Thomas Lamonte Johnson; Jeremy Kane (*Polly*); Collette Kase (*Semtex* and *Ginger*); Norma Kerr (*Cassie*); Wendy Kirby and Stephen Fuller (*Cosi* and *Coco*); Jennie Lodge (*Jake*) Danuta Mayer (*Bilbo,*

*Gyp, Sinann, T.B,* and *Alpha*); John McClenaghan (*Armi*); Alan Menzies; Jan Moore (*Zenobia*); Peter Muswell (*Maisie* and *Prudie*); Marcel and Jane Nassirzadh (*Carlo*); Christopher Netto (*Brewster* and *Tacit*); Ann Marie Donovan O'Neill (*Fionn*); Maria Peploe; Paul and Persephone Pickering; Paolo Pimental (*Islay*); Michael Rasser (*Freddie*); Tim Ridley; Camilla Sampson (*Humphrey* and *Hubert*); Caroline Schroder (*Sprocket*); Scott Simpson (*Jess*); Jane Stevenson (*Henry*); William Thompson; Janice Travell; Jennifer Travell; Sandra Turnbull (*Zen*); John Uncle (*Derby* and *Ziggy*); Doris and Rachael Urqhart (*Lottie* and *Millie*); Peter Waldman (*Sam*); David Ward and Jenny Berry (*Mr. Badger* and *Hattie*); Patricia Holden White (*Quince, Rowan, Damson,* and *Heaven*); Mrs. Wilde (*Emmie*); Mrs. Wood (*Leah*); Chrissie Yggmark (*Morgan*).

Dorling Kindersley also wish to thank Terence C. Bate BVSc, LLB, MRCVS of the RSPCA for his advice on the text; Pedigree Petfoods for supplying equipment and materials; and Aziz Khan for artwork.

Key: t *top*, b *bottom*, c *centre*, l *left*, r *right*, p *panel*

**Photography**
All photographs by Tim Ridley except for:
Bruce Coleman Limited 12tl
Nicholas Goodall 23br, 83, 92, 93 (except p), 99c, 118bl, 118br
Dave King 13pb, 14tr, 14bl, 14-15c, 15cr, 15bl, 93pt, 93pb
Tracy Morgan 14tl, 15t, 15br
David Ward 7br, 9tr, 12c, 13bl, 17c, 17b, 22br, 27br, 82, 84, 85, 90tr, 90tl, 90br, 91p, 93pc, 94tl, 95bl, 102, 108, 109, 112tr, 114br, 116, 117, 125bl, 128t

**Illustrations**
Rowan Clifford 107